1991

Election Coverage

ELECTRONIC MEDIA GUIDES

Election Coverage

Blueprint for Broadcasters

Carla B. Johnston

Focal Press is an imprint of Butterworth–Heinemann.

Library of Congress Cataloging-in-Publication Data
Johnston, Carla B.
    Election coverage: blueprint for broadcasters / Carla B. Johnston
          p.   cm. —(Electronic media guide)
    ISBN 0-240-80088-5 (paperback)
    1. Broadcasting—Political aspects—United States.
    2. Electioneering—United States.
    3. Elections—United States.
    I. Title. II. Series.
    HE8689.7.P6J64 1991
    791.44'658—dc20   90-43779
                                              CIP

British Library Cataloguing in Publication Data
Johnston, Carla B.
    Election coverage: blueprint for broadcasters—(Electronic media guide)
    1. United States. Elections. Campaigns
    I. Title II. Series
    324.73

    ISBN 0-240-80088-5

Butterworth–Heinemann
80 Montvale Avenue
Stoneham, MA 02180

10 9 8 7 6 5 4 3 2 1

Printed in the United States of America

To those broadcasters, candidates, and voters committed to making democratic self-government work.

Contents

Acknowledgments

My purpose in writing this book is to provide a blueprint for broadcasters covering future elections—a positive alternative to the books and articles criticizing past electronic election coverage. A blueprint for election coverage could not be developed without the contributions of many individuals whose diverse talents and concerns advance efforts to achieve structurally sound patterns for action.

Thanks to people working in the broadcast industry: Richard V. Ducey, Senior Vice President, Research and Planning, National Association of Broadcasters, Washington, D.C.; Andrea Mitchell, Chief Congressional Correspondent, NBC News, Washington, D.C.; Emily Rooney, News Director, Andrea Lotoski, Research Director, Jim Gilbert, Assistant Chief Engineer, all of WCVB-TV, Boston; Chuck Crouse, reporter, WEEI-AM Radio, Boston, and columnist for Radio and Television News Directors' Association journal, Washington, D.C.; Eric Johnston, free-lance camera crew for ABC News, New Hampshire primary, 1988; Terry Signaigo, photographer and former editor, WBZ-TV, Boston, and so many others.

Thanks to Commissioner James Quello and Milt Gross, Chief, Equal Time Branch, Federal Communications Commission, Washington, D.C.

Thanks to those who work with broadcast election coverage as candidates, or conveying a client's message, or in analyzing the effectiveness of public policy/ election coverage: former U.S. Senator from Alaska, Mike Gravel; State Representative Diane Wray Williams, District 9a, Minnesota; Merv Weston, Weston Advertising, Manchester, New Hampshire; Daniel Payne, political media consultant, Boston; Ken Swope, Swope and Associates, Boston; Larry Makinson, Project Director, Congress and the Media, Center for Responsive Politics, Washington, D.C.; Robert Manoff, New York University, School of Journalism; and David Schmidt, Initiative Resource Center, San Francisco.

For information about foreign broadcast election coverage, thanks to Peter White, Monash University, Clayton, Victoria, Australia; Australian Broadcast Tribunal; Risto Volanen, Assistant Director for Planning, Finnish Broadcasting Company, Helsinki, Finland; Jens H. Lund, Arhus, Denmark; Frances and George Porter, Wellington, New Zealand; Anders Burholm, Stockholm, Sweden; and Liss Bernstorff, Aabyhoj, Denmark.

Finally, without the confidence of editors Karen Speerstra and Phil Sutherland, the research done by Joan Hill, the vision, creativity, spirit and optimism that civilization can advance provided by my children Elise, Eric, and Debbi, and the unceasing encouragement from Bob Hilliard, the book would never have been completed.

Introduction

Worldwide, the vision of democracy is growing; yet, in the United States "domestic politics has become so shallow, mean and even meaningless that it is failing to produce the ideas and leadership needed to guide the United States."[1]

News commentator David Broder states:

> It would be grotesque at such a moment to watch without protest the strangulation or distortion of democracy in the United States . . .. It is time for those of us in the world's freest press to become activists, not on behalf of a particular party or politician, but on behalf of the process of self-government. It is time to expose the threats to that process and support the efforts to get rid of them.[2]

An opportunity exists to expand creativity in election coverage. Local news is a money maker for stations. Stations are allocating more time to news. "The greatest bang for the buck" for a station is to dare to be different with public affairs and news programming and do some genuine campaign reporting.[3]

Most books on media and elections are oriented to criticism. Very few, if any, provide an electoral coverage blueprint for broadcasters. This book examines the issues, the ethics, and the options for quality electoral coverage within the parameters currently acceptable to American media. My goal is to illustrate that substantive election coverage within news programming is possible, and can advance the debate essential to self-government.

COVERAGE GOALS

Democracy Is Based on Communication

Election broadcasting, according to the Federal Communications Commission, (FCC), is one of the major elements of a station's service "because of the contribution broadcasting can make to an informed electorate—in turn so vital to the proper functioning of our Republic."[4] In fact, expressly for the purpose of preserving democracy, the First Amendment to the U.S. Constitution provides unique protection to this private sector of society: "Congress shall make no law respecting the establishment of religion, or prohibiting the free exercise thereof; or abridging the freedom of speech, or of the press; or the right of the people peaceably to assemble, and to petition the Government for a redress of grievances."

Democracy Requires Participants

Covering elections is different from covering news. News stories require the broadcaster to deal with "audiences—spectators." Election coverage requires the broadcaster to deal with "participants" who will select the officials who determine whether our taxes go up, our take-home pay goes down, and whether or not we benefit from the wide range of public services for which we pay. Self-government can't tolerate a passive "audience": it requires active participation by an engaged electorate. The coverage must enable the listener/viewer to understand how the election decision affects her or him *personally*, and it must leave room for the listener/viewer to "talk back."

An Independent Press

The self-interest of the press has always been to function as the guardian of the public realm. Part of doing this job effectively is enabling the population to see the connections between its participation in elections and the policies that are made, to become "media literate," able to evaluate coverage for itself, and to protect itself— the voters—from being manipulated.

Finding Quality Candidates

Thoughtful, substantive media coverage of all the candidates, their skills, their past records, and the requirements of the jobs they seek to fill can ensure that we hire the best qualified individuals to govern. If we simply allow the campaigner with the biggest megaphone to be arbitrarily designated as "frontrunner," we may not be selecting the person best equipped to govern. The public deserves to have information about all the legally qualified candidates, and about the responsibilities of the jobs.

ELECTION JOURNALISM—NEW TOOLS: NEW APPROACH

Technological advances of recent decades have changed the game for both the media and the candidate. Both are learning how to use their new tools. Computers, satellite news-gathering, graphic tools, and survey research have replaced the campaign trail, the volunteers, issue papers, and pamphlets. The challenge for broadcasters is to use these tools to make election coverage dynamic.

An informed electorate would be "examining public characters and measures," according to James Madison's 1798 vision for democracy. Madison articulated the view of this country's founders that "the people, not the government, possess the absolute sovereignty." Anthony Lewis, *New York Times* columnist, observes that the reality today is far from Madison's vision. Lewis asserts that today "the voters are passive figures in a process utterly remote from public policy, watching shadows on the wall of Plato's cave.[5] This need not be the case. Broadcasting can be a major asset for advancing self-government. Twentieth-century practices have been but an amateur exercise. Twenty-first century broadcasters can employ techniques for effective, fair election coverage, and be mindful of the pitfalls to avoid.

New broadcasters usually have a good idea about how the equipment works. They have begun using their own talents for asking questions, projecting their voices, catching interesting photos, and writing scripts to fit time limits. Nevertheless, veteran radio reporter, Chuck Crouse, is concerned that he still finds people covering elections who don't know about basic government and how it works, and don't even know where to find out about it. In addition, they may not have any background in techniques for applying political science to broadcasting.[6] They may not have realized the need to know about the connections among jobs, people, issues, money, politics, and biases.

In addition, broadcasters need to understand and communicate the news in ways that reflect the ideas of Dr. Robert Manoff of New York University's Journalism Department. He observes that "In campaigns there is no organic relation between the pursuit of ideas and the pursuit of success."[7] Candidates and the media focus on success; concern for issues are "ghetto-ized." A conscientious broadcaster needs to keep in mind the big picture—the advancement of a self-governing society—while reporting on the little picture—who's winning now.

ELECTION COVERAGE MAKES POSSIBLE AN INFORMED ELECTORATE

The Power of the Vote

While it is out of fashion in America to talk about the power of the vote, that power still exists:

1776—one vote gave America the English language instead of German;
1845—one vote brought Texas into the United States;
1868—one vote saved President Andrew Johnson from impeachment;
1875—one vote changed France from a monarchy to a republic;
1923—one vote gave Hitler leadership of the Nazi party;
1941—one vote saved the draft in the United States, just weeks before Pearl Harbor.[8]

Candidates know that they can win or lose by one vote.

Reaching the Voter

Reaching voters is not so difficult in a small town or district where victory requires only 1,000 votes out of a constituency of 1,900 registered voters. But, those who want to be mayors, county commissioners, state legislators, congresspersons, governors, U.S. senators, or president have a more difficult job because they need to reach tens of thousands of voters.

A candidate who runs for U.S. Senate or Governor in a state the size of Florida would need to shake two hands per minute without stop for 24 hours every day for 3 years. A candidate who runs for Mayor in a city of 50,000 voters could shake hands (but not talk) with all the constituents if 8 hours each work day were devoted to nothing else for about 2 months.

Candidates rely on media as the solution to this problem—the way to communicate their message to the majority of voters in their district. They buy advertisements, and they rely on news coverage. They promote their campaigns in any way possible.

THE BLUEPRINT

This book focuses on techniques that enable broadcasters not only to protect their own "First Amendment rights," but also to protect qualified candidates' rights to present their message and credentials, and the voters' rights to understand the responsibilities of the office to which someone will be elected, and to become acquainted with the credentials of all the candidates.

Specifically, the blueprint for coverage is an overlay on the candidates and voters—the subject matter of election coverage—Chapter 1. Chapter 2 and 3 present the issues, options, and techniques useful to management and reporters. Political advertising (Chapter 4) and issue elections (Chapter 5) are designed to identify opportunities for broadcasters. Chapter 6 shows the resources available to broadcasters in polling. Chapter 7, on technology, focuses on the tools available for election coverage. Finally, the book contains reference material on government systems and information sources (Chapter 8) and election laws and regulations (Chapter 9).

Notes

1. Michael Oreskes, "America's Politics Loses Way as Its Vision Changes World," *New York Times*, March 18, 1990, p. 1.
2. David S. Broder, "Democracy and the Press," *Washington Post*, January 3, 1990.
3. Personal interview with Dan Payne, political media consultant, Boston, February 6, 1990.
4. Licensee Responsibility as to Political Broadcasts, 15 FCC 2d 94 (1968); see also Farmers Educational and Cooperative Union of America vs. WDAY, Inc, 360 U.S. 525 (1959); Red Lion Broadcasting Co., Inc, vs. Federal Communications Commission, 395 U.S. 367–94 (1969).
5. Anthony Lewis, "The People Speak," *New York Times*, November 10, 1989, p. A31.
6. Personal interview with Chuck Crouse, reporter, WEEI, Boston (CBS affiliated all-news radio), January 30, 1990.
7. Dr. Robert Manoff, "Power Politics: Reporting the Real Issues," *Media and Values* (Summer/Fall 1988).
8. *Pulse* (publication of the California Human Development Corporation), 1987.

1

Voters, Candidates, and the Media

BROADCASTERS' OBJECTIVES

Media professionals involved in election coverage encounter two groups of people different from the usual business colleague or audience to whom they broadcast—voters and candidates.

Voters rely on the media. They want to elect the best persons; they want to know their options. They don't want government to make their lives more difficult. But most adults find there is little leisure time, and they want to use it for "rest and relaxation," not political education. Consequently, broadcasters' political coverage must find that delicate balance between providing adequate information and enjoyable entertainment in order to teach and hold the average audience.

Candidates want to win. They want coverage—lots of it—preferably favorable. They want to use the media to convince the voters that they should win.

Broadcasters must understand both the voters (as distinct from audiences) and the candidates in order to develop the most effective techniques for handling election coverage. Measuring the candidates against some criteria is the only way to truly assess credentials. You wouldn't hold a public opinion poll to decide the top Olympic athlete. You'd look at standards for excellence. You wouldn't hold a public opinion poll to hire a new news director for your station. You'd measure the applicants against a job description. Why not consider doing that in election coverage?

ANALYSIS FOR THE VOTERS

Credentials Needed for the Job

Often campaigns are covered as races—like sports coverage. Excitement builds and the listener's/viewer's interest is held. But, in nonpolitical races, as Neil Postman[1] points out, the spectators are well aware of the rules of the game—the criteria for top performance. In political races, there are no such criteria, making the process much more subjective. There are some techniques, however, that permit the broadcaster to give his listeners/viewers performance standards for the race. To start with, each public office has a basic job description. The city, town, or county charter lists the credentials for local office. The state or federal constitution will list credentials for positions on those levels. Jobs fall into one of three categories: executive, legislative, and judicial.

Executive Level   If the position to be filled is an *executive* position, the candidate might be measured against general management skills and experience. A manager must be able to organize, to delegate, to monitor performance of others, to make decisions. One need only look at the official budget document for that jurisdiction to identify what the person elected must manage (types of departments, amount of money, number of employees). Obviously, the candidate with some understanding of the issue areas decided by that level of government and expertise in supervising personnel and budgets would be best equipped to handle the job.

Legislative Level   If the position is *legislative*, the candidate might be measured against general skills for being persuasive as a member of a larger group. For example, can the person hold her own in a debate? Is the person able to build consensus or does he operate best as a "loner"? Again, the budget document for that jurisdiction will give the broadcaster some grasp of the range of issues likely to come before the legislative body for new lawmaking and for budget approval

Judicial Level   If the position is *judicial*, the candidate might be measured against general skills for one required to pass judgment on legal cases. Is the person knowledgeable about the law that will be the basis for her decisions? Is the person able to listen? Is the person able to be fair? A review of the type of cases brought before the particular jurisdiction will give the broadcaster added information about the specific issues with which a candidate might be familiar.

Broadcasters can best use these job credentials by providing opportunities for listeners and viewers to measure the credentials of each candidate against the standards required.

Do Elections Affect ME—the Voter?

The Public's Interest   One of the principal reasons given for participation in elections in newly emerging democracies is the empowerment of self-determining how government will "affect me." Conversely, the data about decreased voting in the United States show consistently that people don't participate when they believe it doesn't matter to "me."

The Nonvoters   Curtis Gans, Director of the Committee for the Study of the American Electorate, separates the nonvoters into three blocks: a) those who are poor or minority and are isolated from organized political, social activities; b) 20 million dropouts who "feel that their vote no longer has any efficacy either in improving their lives or the conduct of public policy"; and c) the young who vote in smaller numbers than ever before.

Studies indicate that nonvoters see no difference between the parties, believe that their personal ability to influence government is poor, and find themselves the playthings of chance. The campaign is seen as a device to elect but not to govern. The "here today, gone tomorrow" image candidates are not inspiring to the majority of Americans.[2]

One could say that the voters of America are exercising their right to free speech through their vote. If so, they are voting with their feet. The majority of

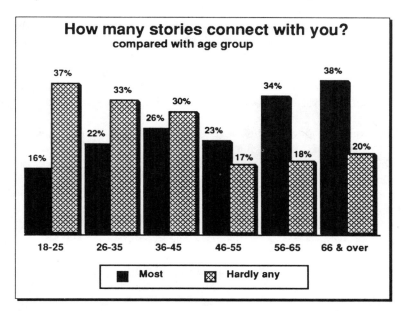

▶ *Figure 1   Relevance of Political Press Coverage. Three-quarters of the people under the age 55 find that press coverage of public issues and political activity has little relevance to their own lives. Even among older audiences whose life experience has provided opportunities to connect public policies with personal lives, the stories do not seem relevant most of the time. The challenge for broadcasters is how to make connections between policy and people's personal lives "real." Source:* Dateline: Capital Hill, *Center for Responsive Politics, Washington, D.C., 1990, p. 25. Report prepared by Larry Makinson.*

Americans are avoiding the polls. In 1988 the nonvoters won: nonvoters, 50%; George Bush, 26.95%; Michael Dukakis, 23.05% [3] In 1986's congressional elections the nonvoters won: nonvoters, 62.7%; Democrats, 18.9%; Republicans,.17%[4]. The United States has the lowest voter participation rate of any advanced democracy in the world. In the last 30 years the level of education is up, the restrictions for voter registration and vote casting have become more lenient, yet the participation in elections continues to decline.[5]

Does the Broadcaster Influence Voter Participation?   Is the broadcaster in any way responsible for educating the listener/viewer about how elected candidates make public policy? In 1987 for the first time the majority of Americans cite TV alone as their main source of news[6]: 66% cite television as their main news source, 36% cite newspapers, 14% radio and 4% magazines. The Roper Report elaborates that the reason for the increased reliance on television is that 55% of the public finds television most believable. Gans observes, "Can we expect public involvement when campaigns are increasingly run on television, inviting citizens to be passive spectators and non-consumers rather than active participants and stockholders in American democracy?"[7]

It would be absurd to blame broadcasters for the decrease in voting. What in fact has happened is that broadcasters, candidates, and voters are learning how to conduct business under the influence of the new technologies available to us. It is like being placed in front of a new computer without being given any instructions about how to make it work effectively. Some of the topics discussed throughout this book focus on how creative broadcasters can use electronic media to enhance participation in elections.

The good news for radio and television broadcasters is that the public (voting and nonvoting) remains interested in politics.

While it is true that people frequently have difficulty connecting politics to their day-to-day personal lives, local news polling indicates consistent interest in politics as a "4" or "5" on a 1-to-10 poll.[8] Politics is an interesting "spectator sport"—but hard to connect to one's personal well-being.[9]

Election Audiences Are Participants, Not Spectators.   Most broadcasters do not use techniques for election coverage that differ from regular news coverage. They have not learned to end the election story without conclusion or opinion, to let the voter decide. Until they learn to do this, the media can undercut the democratic process. For example, studies show that in 1980 "all the media designated losers lost poll support, while all media designated winners gained public opinion strength."[10]

Who stands for the voters' rights? The pattern of traditional news reporting makes it natural to make projections using polling data as if it were "hard news." The candidates have come to understand this. But, if we stop here, we limit our vision for using the new technologies available to us—we unnecessarily limit self-government. Gans states, "The continual withdrawal of the American people from voting and political participation threatens not only wise governance but the underlying vitality of the political process and the democratic ideal."[11]

CANDIDATES

Fears

Public officials facing election campaigns "say they live each day in fear of the four horsemen of modern politics: televised attacks by their opponent, intense personal scrutiny by the press, cynicism on the part of the public, and the need to raise huge sums to buy television time to combat the attacks, scrutiny and cynicism."[12] Candidates at all levels spend each night hearing the four horsemen and planning their "defense." But there is also an "offense" side to the candidate's campaign strategy.

Before the advent of the new technologies, a candidate's strategy involved precinct organizations composed of door-knocking, coffee-sponsoring volunteers. Now, except for the smallest local races (and even they use computerized lists), the "pros" have taken over.

Candidates' "Handlers" and Costs

These pollsters, managers, speech writers, image-makers, and ad agents are charged with the job of "handling" the campaign. First, they identify who will most likely vote for their candidate, and who can be persuaded to do so, so that the candidate will receive a majority of the votes cast. Then they determine what is necessary to please that set of voters. The rest of the campaign is about projecting the desired image and saying the right thing on the right issues—preferably nothing too definitive, lest voters be alienated. The handlers' goal is to remake the candidate into the image that reflects the voters' interests. If a candidate doesn't play this game, the candidate will lose, except in a very small district where personal contact on a substantive level is possible.

Broadcasters need to be aware of the campaign handlers' task in order to adequately do their job of reporting the facts—the facts of the candidate's actual record and credentials, the facts about the campaign's strategy. Broadcasters who are willing to take what is handed to them allow themselves to be reduced to "packager of handlers' pseudo-events," not a reporter of actual events. Reporters must find the time to "scratch the teflon" to preserve a healthy system of checks and balances between campaign handlers and broadcasters.

For the voter and the media, it becomes harder and harder to remember that there may well be a difference between the candidate and the image created by those hired to make the candidate look good.

To support modern sophisticated campaigning requires extraordinary fundraising efforts. The candidate, an individual interested in a career in government, finds herself needing to raise sums that one would expect only an institution or a corporation to raise. The best illustration of this problem is to look at congressional campaign fundraising requirements. The cost of local races have increased in like manner. A U.S. Representative's race would be similar in size to a campaign for an urban Mayor's seat, and a U.S. Senate race would be comparable to that of any state official's campaign. Notice the trends toward increasing costs and the trends that favor incumbents over challengers. (See Figures 2 and 3, pps. 6, 7, and 8.)

In subsequent chapters discussion will focus on techniques available to broadcasters interested in covering campaign finance.

Real versus Pseudo-Events

"Pseudo-events are non-spontaneous activities planted primarily. . . for the immediate purpose of being reported, whose relation to the underlying reality of the situation is ambiguous and whose intention is to be a self-fulfilling prophecy."[13] Pseudo- events are also manifest in staged press conferences, political ads, and are enhanced through the commentary of alleged "experts" on campaigns frequently, called "spin doctors."

Lee Atwater, former Chair of the Republican National Committee, summed up the way many handlers think about creating voter exposure for their candidate. Exposure becomes an obsession—with good reason. It is the key to victory. Atwater explained that the handlers' daily objective is figuring out "what stunt you can pull that will give you fourteen seconds of news hole." To win, a candidate must be heard over the clatter of information and entertainment. Atwater goes on to say that the news media has replaced the political parties; it is so influential in politics and government that it "drives the system."[14]

Spectacle always overwhelms analysis. For example, Michael Deaver, President Reagan's media expert, said that it was far better for Reagan to play the role of starter at the Daytona 500 race than to have him as spectator. This pseudo-event was

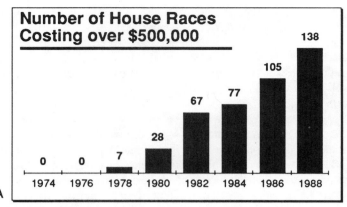

Number of House Races Costing over $500,000

1974: 0
1976: 0
1978: 7
1980: 28
1982: 67
1984: 77
1986: 105
1988: 138

A

▶ *Figure 2*   *Cost of Campaigns. A illustrates the dramatic increase in campaign costs for Congressional races in the 10-year period form 1978 to 1988. As sophicated electioneering techniques—advertising agencies, electronic media ads, polling, direct mail fundraisers, and professional campaign consultants—replace the armies of volunteers licking stamps and knocking on doors in every ward and precinct, campaign costs have escalated enormously. In 1978 only 7 of the 435 congressional races cost over a half-million dollars; in 1988, 138 of those races cost that much.*

the evening-news lead.[15] It certainly beats speeches. Carried to their most bizarre extreme, pseudo-events divert the attention of the American public and the "independent" media from the business of the country to the preservation of candidates who win—and want to keep winning. Two illustrations from Mark Hertsgaard's research of the Reagan White House illustrate how broadcasters can be manipulated by pseudo-events.[16]

Every morning at 8:15 the key Reagan press management staff would meet to choose the "line of the day"—that is, the line they hoped would lead the evening broadcast news and be the headline in the next morning's papers. The choice would be linked to the 3-month strategy focus (for example, the economy). Once selected, it would be woven into the tapestry of the day's events and often be delivered to the press corps in prepackaged form—easy to use. The tactic discourages asking questions on other activities and possibly diverts attention from matters "independent" reporters might be inclined to explore.

The second example is the solution found to the problem that developed when Reagan's cuts in education financing resulted in cuts in his popularity. This was in late 1983; the popularity dip had to be turned around before the 1984 election. Reagan took an "education speech"—the 3Rs, merit pay, excellence—to 25 locations nationwide. The plan was carefully choreographed to assure local evening news coverage in each location. By the end of the period, the 2:1 disapproval of Reagan's education policies reversed itself into a 2:1 approval rating, even though no policy had changed—only the amplification of the rhetoric.

While the above examples focus on national elections, local elections differ only in scale: the candidate's objective is the same—do whatever is necessary to

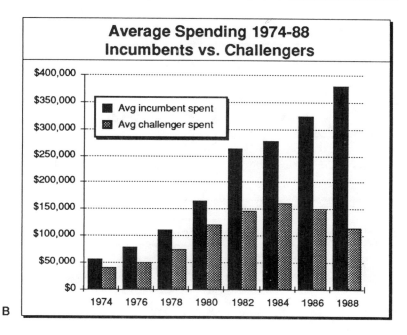

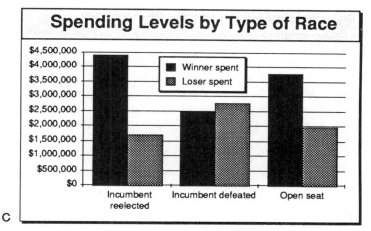

▶ *Figure 2 (continued) B (House spending) and C (Senate spending) illustrate the widening gap between spending by incumbents and spending by challengers. As campaign costs increase, incumbents can raise money more easily. An incumbent is a better investment for a donor because by and large, the biggest spender wins. Source: Larry Makinson,* The Price of Admission, *Washington, D. C.: Center for Responsive Politics, 1989, pp. 11 and 19.*

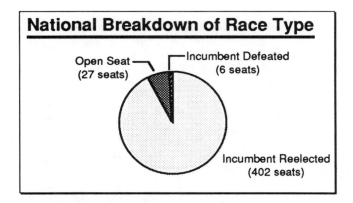

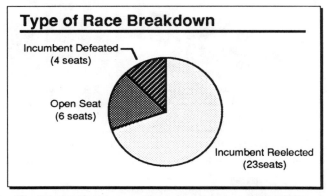

▶ *Figure 3   The Permanent Congress Charts showing the result of high-priced campaigning where fewer and fewer challengers can compete financially—a permanent Congress. In
1988, 402 of the 408 House members who ran for reelection won. That is 98.5%. 23 of the 27
Senators who ran for reelection won. That is 85%. Historically, challengers won more
frequently. (Note: Every one of the 435 House members stands for election every two years.
One-third of the 100 Senators stand for election every two years. A Senator serves a 6-year
term.) Source: Larry Makinson, The Price of Admission (Washington, D.C.: Center for
Responsive Politics, 1989). p. 19 and 29.*

get the media coverage required for exposure to the voters. One technique broadcasters can employ to avoid becoming captive by campaign handlers is to follow a
preestablished campaign coverage plan that provides a mechanism for independent
reporting to supplement the daily campaign news. Such campaign plans are discussed in Chapter 3.

The Candidate's Objective

Not all candidate releases are "created images." However, whether the candidate releases a poll or a press release, makes a public appearance, decides the content
and placement of a political advertisement—everything has a calculated purpose;
win. While the broadcaster must avoid being manipulated, he also has a responsibil-

ity to help the voter familiarize herself or himself with each of the candidates. That requires providing a balance of opportunities for the candidates to communicate their campaign message without commentary. It requires understanding the campaign handlers' job—enabling a candidate to communicate effectively to his or her constituents. It requires a firm resolve to ask the hard questions, but not to embark upon a "witch hunt."

One technique for the broadcaster seeking to balance the coverage is to allow all the candidates freedom and time to communicate their message in their own format on at least two occasions—when they announce, and a day or so before election day. On other occasions, after asking the hard questions, broadcast the candidates' reply, not the interpretation of commentators.

Candidates and Ads

Another part of the candidate's strategy is to reach the "right" voters through advertisements. As with product advertising, candidate ads are carefully placed. Target buying, done by the campaign handlers, involves calculated decisions about ad location, time, length, and vehicle. The public ought to understand who is being targeted and why. Broadcasters, as the independent guardian of the public realm, have both the responsibility and the opportunity to tell the story behind the advertisement—the campaign's strategy. This can be done in several ways. Comparing ads with voter records is one option. Another is to do stories about district demographics and campaign targeting of selected population groups.

One problem for both the candidate and the voter is how to ensure truth in advertising. If a candidate is smeared, there is no one to referee. Advertisers don't pay a price for lying or making things up. How will the public ever hear the full story? If investigative reporting finds that a given advertisement contained a lie or a distortion of the truth, one item on the news can't begin to compensate for the repetition of the negative ads. The only alternative for a candidate is to raise money to buy ads to respond to smears. To do this, the candidate may lose the opportunity to place constructive ads because of limits on either available advertising slots or money. Stories comparing actual records with advertising claims or charges can help correct distortion and smears.

Political media consultant Dan Payne says that journalists haven't covered advertising much because they don't understand it. A broadcast ad depends on repetition. It must be on the air dozens of times to be remembered, whereas a broadcast journalist works on the assumption that repetition is sloppy—"we did that story yesterday." [17]

THE TAIL WAGGING THE DOG

Veteran reporter and NBC Chief Congressional Correspondent Andrea Mitchell states:

> I've covered campaigns since '68 and national campaigns since '72 and all conventions and I'm struck by how we're losing this battle against the media handlers and campaign managers who become so adept at knowing our deadlines, our desire for good pictures, what makes best 'photo op' and how to design

a political ad which is synergistic with the so-called free media that they expect to get on our news casts daily. [18]

If a candidate feels that she is ahead, the campaign cuts contact with reporters, cuts news conferences, cuts opportunities to question the candidate, and relies on highly stylized commercials that fit in with the candidate's overall image—a complete and unified packaging. The only alternative for the broadcaster is to develop an agenda of issues for coverage over the course of the election, and a plan for doing it. This way broadcasters can ensure that they won't be manipulated by either the candidates or the horse-race zealots (the pollsters), even when deadlines are tight and materials are short.

In developing this agenda, broadcasters can learn a lot from those familiar with the bridge between political science and the media. Bob Beckel, a 1984 Mondale campaign handler who acquired press credentials in 1988 and played political analyst says, "Except for a few, [most journalists] don't know politics from chicken soup."[19] However, to preserve unbiased coverage, free from manipulation by any political camp, broadcast management must develop a coverage plan that draws on the skills of these individuals who "play both sides of the street" but does not allow them to color the fairness of the station's coverage and does not allow their commentary to preempt the voter's right to make independent decisions.

Notes

1. Neil Postman, *Amusing Ourselves to Death* (New York: Penguin Books, 1985), 125.
2. Walter Dean Burnham, "Electing Not To," *Boston Globe*, September 6, 1987, p. 29.
3. M.K. Frisby, "Vote-Turnout Rate the Second Lowest of 20th Century," *Boston Globe*, November 11, 1989, p. 17.
4. Curtis Gans, quoted in "Picking a President," *Washington Spectator* 13, no. 10 (May 15, 1987): 2.
5. Austin Ranney, *Channels of Power: The Impact of Television on American Politics* (New York: Basic Books, 1983).
6. The Roper Organization, *America's Watching*. New York: Television Information Office, 1990.
7. Gans, in "Picking a President."
8. Personal interview with Emily Rooney, news director, WCVB-TV, Boston, March 5, 1990.
9. Ranney, *Channels of Power*, 70 ; also National Opinion Research Center, "General Survey for February–April, 1982," *Public Opinion* (October/November 1982): 28.
10. W.C. Adams, ed. *Television Coverage of the 1980 Presidential Election Campaign* (Norwood, NJ: Ablex, 1983), 58.
11. Gans, in "Picking a President."
12. Michael Oreskes, "America's Politics Loses Way as Its Vision Changes World," *New York Times,* March 18, 1990, p. 1.
13. See Dr. Manny Paraschos, "Abstract: Network Coverage of the 1988 Bush Ambush of Boston: A Challenge to the Traditional Definition of News" (Boston: 1989). The text material is taken from a Paraschos reference to D. Boorstin *The Image* (New York: Atheneum, 1985), 11–12.

14. Oreskes, "America's Politics Loses."
15. Bill Moyers, "In the Public Mind," WGBH-TV, Boston, November 22, 1989.
16. Mark Hertsgaard's lecture on his book, *On Bended Knee,* Institute for Policy Studies Conference, Amsterdam, The Netherlands, 1990. Tape.
17. Personal interview with Dan Payne, political consultant, Boston, February 6, 1990.
18. Personal interview with Andrea Mitchell, Chief Congressional Correspondent, NBC News, Washington D.C., February 14, 1990.
19. Jules Whitcover, "Working Both Sides of the Street," *Boston Globe*, April 8, 1990, p. A 22.

2

▼
▼
▼
▼

Broadcast Management and Election Coverage Plans

REMEMBER THE GOAL

Mark Twain said, "There are only two forces that can carry light to all corners of the globe—the sun in the heavens and the Associated Press." Today, we might expand that to include all the media—broadcast, especially.

To most of us that "light" is the concept of democracy—self-government, freedom, human rights. We in the United States often are better at looking out the window at the rest of the world than we are at looking in a mirror, at ourselves. But most broadcasters would share the views of Richard Ducey, Director of Research and Planning at the National Association of Broadcasters, when he says, "We all know an informed democracy is important." [1]

Television has become the great democratizer—the vehicle for enabling all America, in fact, the whole world, to participate in a common experience. The whole world was there when the Berlin Wall came down. The whole world watched. Owners, station managers, bureau chiefs, news directors and, those in management positions in stations have many things to think about in planning election coverage. The bottom line is how to do one's best for the well-being of the democratic system while not sacrificing ratings, profits, and time lost in legal hassles and controversy.

At a busy station, election coverage may well get lost in the bureaucracy—ads, news, public affairs, community programming, and so on. There's no particular employee charged with being the public guardian of democracy for the station. Not even the director of the political unit can do this alone, even if the station can afford the luxury of such a unit.

STATION MANAGEMENT AND A CAMPAIGN COVERAGE PLAN

Beware the "Ad Hoc-ery of Expedience"

Broadcasters face a unique opportunity and challenge in handling election coverage. The best and the brightest will devise ways to satisfy their audience without trivializing elections, that is, to differentiate between an election campaign and a sitcom—and keep the audience. Here's where a well-thought-out plan pays off.

Ad hoc decisionmaking too often has prevailed. It has often been difficult to do otherwise because a) broadcast management feels itself at the mercy of FCC regulation (and anticipated regulation), b) bad-mouthing and mud-slinging seem to dominate candidates' activities, c) broadcasters are concerned about the audience's real interest in politics, and d) a generalist in management may sometimes feel "at sea" about the judgment calls governing the intricacies of political science, government jurisdictional issues, and political manipulation. Yet, the lack of a plan usually perpetuates headaches.

Often only the networks and the largest of stations have been able to assign staff to develop a "plan" for their election season. If your station cannot allocate staff time for developing a plan from "scratch," consider hiring a consultant to develop such a plan tailored for your station and your situation, or consider drawing on the ideas in this book. Ideally, one would develop a plan a year to 18 months ahead of the election, depending on the type of election. If staff time and resources are short, one could develop a "master plan" and use it, with modifications, for all elections. The message is that *any* plan is better than no plan: a carefully developed plan best serves the station, the voters, and the candidates.

Issues for a Campaign Coverage Plan

An informed democracy requires "literate" participants in the political process, not an audience believing democracy is a spectator sport. How can the station's coverage encourage "media literacy" so that listeners and viewers can develop their "talking back" skills? People must understand issues such as distortion, blackouts, unsubstantiated polls, and the limits to commentary—issues covered later in this book.

To develop a station plan for campaign coverage, broadcast management begins by identifying the criteria that can be used to measure effective coverage. Find answers to the following questions:

1. What kind of coverage is needed for your station to be the independent voice that the Constitution intended?
2. What types of skills are needed for effective campaign reporters?
3. What awards might your station seek as recognition for quality election coverage?
4. How can your station be effective and stretch limited resources to the maximum?
5. Will you cover the story of campaign advertising as equally important as campaign "photo ops"? (photo opportunity—a striking photo or live action sequence that the news media find attractive)
6. Can you cover state and local campaigns the same way federal campaigns are covered? Is that desirable?
7. Will you develop station policies concerning ads and make them available in writing?
8. How much time will be given to each race and ballot issue and how will it be allocated? What happens to the plan when the "photo op" of the day competes?
9. How will your station handle *issue* elections? They are different from public service campaigns and different from candidate elections. Even controversial items deserve coverage if the voter will be required to pass judgment on them. How can that be done without repercussions?

10. What is the best way for the station to allocate reporter time between the candidate "on the campaign trail" and independent investigative reporting?
11. How will you allocate coverage between the primary and the general election? All too often we forget that a decision critical to the election may not be on election day—it happens months before when those few who pay attention contribute to deciding who will or won't be official candidates. The preprimary period is often insufficiently covered; yet it is the most critical period in democratic selection—the determination of what choices are possible.
12. Will you treat every level of office and every qualified candidate with equal time?
13. How will you use polling data?
14. Are there any judgment calls to call to the attention of station employees?
15. What new options are possible because of technological advances? Consider uses for computer graphics, satellite news, viewer-response options.

The answers to these questions emerge in the process of developing the station's campaign coverage plan. This chapter focuses on developing such a plan. The rest of the book will address the answers to the above questions.

Criteria for Hiring a Consultant to Develop Your Plan

Small stations who decide to hire a consultant to develop a campaign plan should require that the plan be completed 10 months before the next election cycle. For maximal usefulness to the station, the scope of work for the consultant should involve several things: 1) format suggestions should be developed for each level race your station will be covering; 2) the budget for each component of proposed coverage should be developed in a way that the station can easily substitute updated figures in future years; 3) the plan should be accompanied by an implementation time line identifying who must do what, and when to carry out the plan; and 4) resources for reporter research should be specified in the plan, addresses, phone numbers, and perhaps computerized files, so that the reporter responsible for election coverage can easily do the kinds of investigative research that enhance the coverage.

The firm or person hired to develop this plan should have had political and government experience; however, it is imperative that it be someone who is not active politically at the time the firm undertakes this work for the station. In addition, it should be someone who understands the broad responsibility of a station to facilitate an informed democracy—not someone who has a narrower view from experiences as campaign manager, candidate media advisor, or pollster.

Doing One's Own Plan

A Network Point of View Network coverage is for the presidential campaign, and the major congressional and gubernatorial races. A local station can learn from the thinking about campaign coverage at this level, and the key ingredient: money. In the 1988 presidential campaign each of the networks spent about $30 million.

A good chunk of the network time went to convention coverage, an area where future cutbacks in expenditures are likely. With the increasing emphasis on primary elections, the convention often is just exaggerated advertisement for each party. Often it is all charade.[2] The nomination vote allocation may be known already. The platforms are written in advance (with little coverage of the real platform-drafting debate between candidates in the Party).[3] For networks, convention coverage takes on a form of self-promotion, anchor enhancement and career development for star correspondents. Thoughtful network planners are asking whether the costs of convention coverage outweigh the benefits to the voters, the candidates, and the networks.

The more fundamental question is, how can the networks do a better job of informing and challenging people?. Timothy J. Russert, Senior Vice-President and Washington Bureau Chief of NBC News, suggests five ways that presidential campaign coverage can be improved. He directs the suggestions at the networks, but local stations covering races at any level can also benefit from the suggestions:

1. *A stump speech* for each candidate should be carried in its entirety, early in the campaign. This is the way a candidate chooses to present himself to the voters. The message deserves to be heard. The message should be analyzed for accuracy and acuity.

2. *"Photo Ops"* should be used only as introductory news peg for a substantive report—that is, link George Bush in Boston Harbor with his environmental record and link Michael Dukakis in the army tank with his position on defense. "The staging would stop. The campaigns would instead spend their time developing and distinguishing their positions on the issues."

3. *Campaign planes* should not hold the seasoned reporters hostage to the flying sideshow. They should be home researching the important news stories. The same could be said for campaign buses or caravans in state and congressional elections.

4. *Commercials* should be dissected and analyzed regularly to hold candidates accountable for truth in advertising. "The knowledge that every image and word will be scrutinized will immediately improve any politician's behavior."

5. *Debates* should be sponsored by each of the four major networks, ABC, CBS, CNN, and NBC, moderated by their own anchors. The moderator's only role would be to change the subject, clarify differences, and keep order. The first three debates would each focus on one topic: economic policy, social policy, and foreign policy. The final debate would cover issues and differences that had emerged during the campaign. If a candidate chose not to appear, the debate would go forward with an empty chair. "No one candidate will cede his or her opponent unilateral access to an audience of 70 million people."[4]

Station Plans: The Local Television Viewpoint   Local television news can borrow from the network approach to a campaign coverage plan, but the demands of a local audience require some different approaches. WCVB TV Boston (a Hearst station and an ABC affiliate) provides a good example of campaign coverage planning. In fact, WCVB-TV won the Edward R. Murrow Award for Continuing Coverage for their 1988 election coverage—quite a feat when continuing coverage awards usually go to dramatic events such as hurricanes, fires, and murders.

A videotape introducing the station's plan states, "Our coverage was designed to be different, and, to make a difference. In the past, sometimes the candidates won. They beat us. They were two steps ahead of us. We didn't have a plan. In 1988 we had a plan and we stuck to it."[5] The plan had several components designed to provide substantive coverage and be responsive to candidates, but to avoid manipulation by campaign handlers:

1. *Introductory candidate interviews* were held individually with each eligible candidate at the very beginning of the campaign. Each interview lasted 1 to 1½ hours and was a taped record of the candidate's position on various issues. "These interviews gave us incredible mileage. We used and reused them in our series of issues pieces. And, if a candidate changed their position, we had the record."[6]

2. *Twenty-five issue pieces* analyzed key issues in depth and in length, and, in the final weeks before the election, reexamined the surviving candidates' views on issues.

3. *Five American families* were selected to represent a cross-section of the population trying to decide which candidate was best. The criteria was that families selected must be articulate, diverse, independent or completely noncommitted. Initially, a profile was done, and at appropriate intervals reporters "checked in" for an update on their views. This local station had a hometown candidate for President, Michael Dukakis, so it selected families from across the United States and used its membership in the CONUS network (see Chapter 7) to facilitate coverage for the Boston local news. This approach could be adapted by a local station covering a state or local campaign.

4. *Nine key states* were brought into the spotlight—WCVB's way of making a hometown candidate more than a hometown story. The states selected were ones with a lot of electoral votes and "swing states" where party preference was unclear.

In addition to these special types of coverage, the station covered the regular news stories, and "tarmac" press conferences, conducted its own polling through a cooperative of CONUS stations and the services of the Gallup polling organization (a way to make it affordable for a local station), and covered the debates and the conventions. Station News Director Emily Rooney states that one of the hardest parts of the plan was sticking to the plan. To do justice to many of the stories required five minutes or more on the 6 P.M. news. "It's hard some mornings, when a key story is a homicide or a truck accident, to argue that in addition to 'the *sound-bite* of the day,' we should make time for the political issue we had pre-planned. But, we did it."[7]

In January 1987, the station began to develop its plan for covering the presidential election that would culminate in November 1988. The ideas were matched with a range of budget options—options that would change depending on the options for coverage and on the fortunes of the hometown candidate.[8] WCVB-TV found that politics is always fourth or fifth on the "top ten" lists of viewer interests. Building on the extent of this interest, the station designed a plan in which political coverage could be included within the 4½ hours of news programmed each day, plus, in some cases, add special programming. As a rule, two out of the nine pieces in their evening news—occasionally as many as four—would be political.

The submission for the Murrow award summarized the station's accomplishment as follows: "Our approach was different. News Center 5 went beyond the sound-bites to get our viewers involved in the selection of a President. There is no way that someone who watched the preponderance of our coverage could not have been reasonably well informed on this campaign."[9]

Local Radio Station Plans   News and information formats made strong gains in radio markets in 1989.[10] Opportunity exists for radio news to benefit from well-designed election plans. Some radio stations can afford to develop elaborate plans a year ahead. But in a small station with three or less reporters, contacting party organizations and campaign officers, reading position papers, doing investigative reporting, following the campaign schedules, and planning special coverage takes more time and staff than available. If yours is such a station, you still might want to talk about what is possible, planning a year before the elections. Once your plan is in place, it can be modified for use each successive year. In developing the plan, remember, the real choices come early—convention and primary time. You might follow the WCVB approach or hire someone to develop a detailed blueprint that you can implement each year based on your resources.

Some of the possibilities for small radio station campaign coverage plans are:

1.   Meet with other stations and newspapers to collaborate on certain aspects of campaign coverage. For example, a combined computer base could provide everyone access to incumbent voting records, campaign positions, campaign finance data, demographic data, and election history for the district.

2.   Stations might collaborate on an initial-in-depth interview with all candidates to discuss their credentials and their viewpoint. Segments of such tapes could be used throughout the campaign. Such interviews might take a half day's work very early in the campaign, but they would enable the small station to have useful material readily available for several months.

3.   A standard set of criteria against which listeners could measure candidate credentials might be developed collaboratively with other stations and newspapers. This "job description" for each elective position in the station's market could then be used in future years.

Large-market radio stations, especially those with all-news or heavy news formats, are able to develop detailed campaign coverage plans. WEEI, Boston, is a model of a large radio station: a CBS affiliate, it has a staff of 30 people. This local radio station decided to invest early in the 1988 presidential campaign. It sent a reporter with Michael Dukakis, the Massachusetts Governor, on Dukakis's exploratory trip across the country designed to determine whether or not the Governor should run for president. This coverage gave strong credibility to the radio station. Listeners are impressed when you are out in the field. Station ratings go up. Advertisers like the proactive role. Staff members find it an exciting place to work. And the corporate ego is satisfied because the station can say, "We're out doing things."[11]

Adapting Your Plan for Different Election Levels

The discussion thus far has focused primarily on national elections, because it is at that level at which we all have a common experience. But both network and local station coverage plans can be adapted to state, county, and local elections. In fact, once your station has a plan, modifying it each year to any given level is relatively easy.

For example, in the case of the 1990 state elections, the local television station presented earlier, WCVB-TV, began about a year in advance to adapt their national campaign plan. Charles Kravetz, Director of the 1990 Political Unit, described the plan:

1. *"Political Breaking News"* from each campaign would be reported daily.
2. *"Inside the Campaigns and Candidates"* would be a series on personalities, organizations and issues 'behind the scenes' 'on the campaign trail.'
3. *"The Main Streets of Massachusetts"* ' would be a weekly series focusing on issues facing a given community and how that community looks at the candidates.[12]

In addition to the above, the station developed a schedule of priorities for special coverage:

1. *Mini-debates* between candidates on the six o'clock newscasts. These might be 5 minutes long, or less. Frequency would increase as elections near.
2. *Convention coverage* would be limited.
3. *"Election '90 Sunday"* would be a weekly program to run from 5:00 to 5:30 P.M. live to address issues and events making election news. A given program could include a "set-up piece," candidate interviews, pundits, and a roundtable with a local anchor or reporter serving as host.
4. *Major debates* would be covered in newscasts, and the station would sponsor and broadcast live several debates.
5. *Polling* would continue in collaboration with other area news organizations.[13]

GOOD RATINGS: WHAT DOES THE LISTENER/VIEWER WANT?

Arthur Nielsen, founder of Nielsen Media Research, a leading ratings organization, has stated, "Since what the broadcaster has to sell is an audience to advertisers—the broadcaster must cater to the public tastes and preferences. . . . To be successful an advertiser must find out which programs appeal to potential customers, and then select the program that reaches that audience at the lowest cost. This is the purpose and function performed by the Nielsen Ratings."[14]

Back in the 1960s and 1970s news coverage was an economic loser for a station. Things have changed dramatically in the last few years. News is expanding, and for many local stations, it is a key income factor. First, it is cheaper to produce local news than it is to produce or buy entertainment shows. Second, news became much more interesting in the mid-1970s when live mini-camera electronic news-gathering, (ENG), was introduced. Third, in the mid-1980s, with the advent of satellite news-gathering, (SNG), the viewer can "be anywhere—live." News is no longer "talking heads." It has become much more exciting and even entertaining.

Aside from the generalizations about more favorable reaction to news coverage, what do we know about how much listeners/viewers like election coverage? Nielsen did a special report on the 1984 presidential election, focusing on network coverage. In 1984 (and in 1980) the national conventions were watched most by women and men over 50. College-educated people and upper-income groups watched most, as did those who were not subscribers to pay cable. Election night activity attracts higher audiences—in the 1984 presidential race, 5% higher than on a typical Tuesday. Again, women and people of both sexes over 50 watch the most election coverage. Those under 35 watch the least. The Nielsen conclusions were that "politics continues to be regarded as attractive program fare by the nation's TV viewers. More than 70% and occasionally over 90% of TV households have tuned to conventions and election results for each of the last seven presidential elections."[15]

At a local rating level, little exists that relates specifically to elections. But local monitoring of ratings is becoming increasingly sophisticated.[16] In larger markets now, a daily printout is available showing the ratings for the previous 24 hours by 15-minute segments. In smaller markets this material is gathered at four to seven intervals throughout the year. The Arbitron Ratings Company introduced its ScanAmerica service, test-marketed in the mid-1980s. This service couples an electronic tracking of household television viewing with portable UPC scanners to record product purchases. Station sales personnel, planners, and advertising agency account managers can identify exactly where to place a spot for a given product and determine how many spots are needed to accumulate the desired number of gross rating points necessary to reach sufficient viewers to sell a given quantity of the product. Candidates are not yet being sold to voters with quite the level of precision that commercial products are sold, but national campaigns are approaching this level. It is likely that local candidates will be sold to specific voting groups through television-spot placement. Studies are available to campaign media buyers that indicate programs watched by those who have previously worked for political candidates, and programs watched by those most likely to vote. The broadcast manager should build this information into the station's campaign coverage plan.

Station management is to a great extent governed by how the local ratings affect the purchase of advertising for its programs. The coverage of elections, per se, falls within this overall mosaic. The creative broadcaster needs to look beyond the statistics. While these statistics provide a snapshot of the audience at a given point in time and a tally of the number of hours of coverage of given events, they do not provide the detail needed to determine why some political programming brings better ratings than other programming, and why certain times, or certain elections, are deemed more important by the voter than others. The creative broadcaster can find ways to provide valuable election coverage, while simultaneously addressing the self-interests of the viewers/listeners and the news ratings for the station.

STATION FINANCES AND ELECTION REVENUE

In the last 10 years, as noted above, local news has grown as a revenue center. Not only does local news draw good audiences, but compared to the high costs for other program formats, news is relatively economical to produce. For example, the Walt Disney Company recently bought a Los Angeles station, and to the surprise of many, instead of running Disney movies, it is concentrating on local news. The biggest money-maker in broadcast television is "60 Minutes." It costs peanuts to make, and it brings in big bucks. The cost of not generating high ratings—usual for news shows—is offset by a tremendous return on investment. In addition, increased competition from cable, and VCRs is shrinking the audience share for broadcasters so broadcasters lose ratings. More sources are competing for programming. If I want to buy shows for my station, I must compete with cable stations. Then, too, in 1970 there were a few dozen independent stations. Today there are 360 independents competing for programs. The demand increases but the supply is relatively the same; consequently, costs rise. Programs are more expensive. Audience share is declining and everyone is looking for niches. Local television and radio can do local news best. It's the right product for cost-conscious times.[17]

Aside from news revenues, elections bring in revenue from campaign advertising. In 1988, just under 1% of net revenue for FM radio stations came from political ads. For AM radio the figure was just under 2% of revenue. For affiliated TV stations, 3.6% of net revenues was received from political advertising, and for independent television stations the total was 1.6% of net revenues. Network figures were not available.[18]

CHOOSING TONE

Part of developing a campaign coverage plan is being sensitive to the tone of coverage—that is, the feeling or attitude conveyed to the audience with the information. It is important to avoid broadcasting material that discriminates or distorts. Certain areas must be considered as one establishes the appropriate tone for coverage:

Trivializing

Some suggest that campaigns are trivialized because reporters are ignorant on substance and therefore cannot ask the right questions concerning policy, nor can they analyze candidates' response except by reference to its political impact.[19] This is not the case when a station develops a suitable election coverage plan. The investigative data will be computer-accessible. The sequence of programming will interrelate the 30-second to 3-minute pieces with the "in-depth" pieces, and with coverage that allows a different perspective. The station will have developed suitable collaboration between all three mediums—radio, television, and newsprint. The plan will allow the substance to be addressed in carefully selected formats.

Modern campaigns have changed dramatically, yet coverage is much as it was in the 1960s. Many programs still rely on "talking heads" and carry the "canned stuff" prepared for them by campaign media consultants. The press has to cover what is important. Be careful of the claim that candidates must show the broadcaster what's news so that the broadcaster can deliver it to the audience without change. The problem is that the electronic press can easily be manipulated by those who are skilled at perfecting the most memorable sound-bite (a short dramatic catch-phrase that attempts to capture the essence of the candidates statements) or the most dramatic image; candidates spend most of their money and much of their time providing the electronic media with the sound-bites and images that make them—the candidates—look most favorable. Sometimes objective reporting and the analysis can fall between the cracks. Carefully selected formats for coverage can rectify any such distortion or omission.

Judgment Calls

Management must be aware of the subtleties of judgment made by a range of station employees in covering elections. These overlay the content, whatever the format, and the judgments can preempt the voter's right to assess and chose the best candidate. What are some of these judgments?

Visual versus Verbal   In television the visual always overrides the verbal. As Bill Moyers says, "spectacle overwhelms analysis."[20] Consider carefully how images can be both vivid and accurate portrayals of each campaign. One technique for achieving this goal is to know your candidate, the message of the campaign, and the track record of the individual. Then, measure the validity of the visual against this information to ensure that your visual is an accurate portrayal of the campaign. Beware of broadcasting the most dramatic visual for its own sake. Electing policy-makers requires different standards from selecting photo-contest winners. But, with luck and thought one can broadcast visuals that are both accurate and dramatic.

Management Bias   As in all organizations, employees learn to conform to what they believe to be the management bias on politics. It is important that management provide directives about how employees are to handle controversial aspects of election coverage. Bias is all right, but it belongs in editorials. Fairness and full coverage are the measures for quality broadcasting. The best technique for dealing with controversy is to face it squarely. For example, rather than avoiding discussion of issues like abortion, lest it upset the audience, invite the audience to present its views. Encourage free speech. *Listen* to the prevailing themes emerging from audience response. Look at your market analysis studies and base future programming on the issues of greatest interest to your audience. Question the candidates on the same audience concerns.

To accomplish such fair and full coverage, management must encourage its employees not to avoid any issues, but to cover the viewpoints of opposing sides and the reasons for these viewpoints. Otherwise, employees, in a self-interest move to protect their own careers, will either broadcast the information they believe to be consistent with management's view, or, to be safe, sanitize the coverage and avoid legitimate debate.

Conformity versus Innovation   Stations worried about losing audience to rivals and stations with the lowest ratings in their market have little to lose and much to gain by trying innovative coverage. Unfortunately, management of marginal stations sometimes extends their caution to new formats and creative ideas, thus preventing their own resurgence.

Value Judgments: Tiers, Wealth, Hiring   Value judgments often influence the objectivity of election coverage. Emphasis on these matters at the neglect of what the candidate stands for and what the candidate's skills are deprives the viewer of full information. In addition, every person preparing material for broadcast frequently makes decisions laden with value judgments that may not even be conscious determinations:

1. *Tiers*   Choosing to cover only "top candidates" or to cover candidates in station-determined "tiers" inadvertently and inappropriately closes voter options. No one has the right to engage in segregation. Election laws determine who is legally qualified to be on the ballot. Anyone who meets these criteria (usually a threshold of signatures from registered voters) deserves the right to be presented to the voters in a fair and equal way. This can be done by ensuring that the formats selected for programs offer equal exposure in comparable time slots.

2. *Wealth*   Sometimes candidates are emphasized or deemphasized based on the money spent by their campaign to buy name recognition, which translates into visibility on polls, which translates into free media coverage, which translates into more name recognition. In a democratic society, if we don't want to end up with "the best government money can buy," it is important to provide full and equal coverage to all legal candidates regardless of wealth. A useful technique for handling this is to build into the station campaign plan a) *time* for all the candidates, b) *focus* on credentials and experience that emphasizes capability, and c) "infotaining" items on *each* candidate to counteract the celebrity status resulting from wealth.

3. *Hiring*   A critical judgment for management concerns staff. Once the station develops a plan, the key to success, according to FCC Commissioner Jim Quello, a former manager of a Detroit radio station, is to hire good employees—employees who represent in themselves a balance of the society, because "election coverage requires a delicate balance."[21] The criteria for employment must include a) evidence of ability to present diverse viewpoints equitably, b) interest and skill in researching a story in order to present independent and accurate information, c) an openness to learning coupled with an ability to understand the dynamics of institutions, politics, and personal motivations, and d) an ability to separate personal bias and cynicism from one's work.

CHOOSING FORMATS

The tone of a station's coverage is the base for its political plan, but the packaged formats are the vehicles for carrying the message to the public. A station plan that incorporates a range of program formats can have more versatile and more interesting coverage. Monitoring ratings will indicate which formats are most appealing to the public. Formats commonly used for election coverage include news, debate, and special coverage format.

News Formats

Election coverage makes the best news when it can be tailored to fit the common definition of news: "The news value of an event can be judged by its *impact* or *consequences*, whether the event is *unusual* and whether the people involved in the event are well-known or *prominent*." In addition, factors contributing to news value include *conflict*, *proximity* to audience, *timeliness* (do people still care?)."[22]

Roper polls show that the public likes television news. By the mid-1980s national news broadcasts became moderately profitable, but local news was much more profitable. That's because the local station has a loyal audience, can have more sports, more human interest, more "how to do it" coverage.[23]

One example of highlighting the election coverage plan within the local news broadcast is the following 5-minute news segment. Just before the Republican State Convention in 1990, WCVB ran a 5-minute segment on its "six o'clock news."[24] The first visual was the station's "Election '90" logo. This was followed by a visual of the candidates talking while the reporter introduced the story. Next the screen showed a computer graphic, listing each candidate, an issue, and if the candidate favored or opposed the issue. Some campaign-action visuals followed with the reporter stating that three issues were particularly important. A computer graphic identified each of the three by name. Then three graphics followed giving candidate position on each of the three. The reporter signed off.

The problems solved by using such a format include a) cohesiveness of all election broadcasts under a common "logo," b) use of visuals to communicate substance—computer-graphic visuals, c) dedication of enough time for a segment to present alternative views on a single issue—say, 5 minutes, and d) integration of elections with hard news to reinforce the fact that selection of public policy-makers does determine the type of policy made. An election is not a sideshow divorced from "real" news.

Debate Formats

Another common campaign format is the debate. Debates are almost certainly a part of a presidential campaign. And, at a congressional district level, the National Association of Broadcasters (NAB) reports that virtually all races have a broadcast debate.[25] The format is used widely for more local races, too. In 1984 NAB surveyed television news directors and determined that 45% offered to sponsor debates for local, state, or federal candidates for office. In 1986, the number making this offer increased to 56.1%.[26] The debates that were carried were not just for national office. In 1984, 41% carried debates for local candidates. In 1986, 46.2% did so. The office for which candidates were offered debate time were Congress, 40.3% of the offers; Governor, 36.3% of the offers; State Legislature, 17.8%; and city/county offices, 17.5%.

However, providing the voter the opportunity to hear the candidate cannot be done by the broadcaster alone. The NAB survey found that 55.4% of the stations that offered debate time in 1984 were refused at least once by one of the candidates. In 1986, 45.3% had the same experience.

The most important consideration concerning debates is that of debate format. One option is a round table seating the candidates and a news anchor who says little. In 1984, in New York's democratic primary, a debate like this was moderated by Dan Rather, providing a one-on-one for Fritz Mondale, Gary Hart, and Jesse Jackson. This is also the format suggested earlier in this chapter for 1992 network planning. This format has the advantage of letting the listener/viewer evaluate the candidate's thoughtfulness, substantive ideas, presentation style, and his/her ability to listen to others. The presentations are not cloaked in tight guidelines that camouflage the candidate's own ability and style.

Another option is the two-podium approach with a bank of reporters selected to ask specific questions. The 1988 election paired Lloyd Bentsen and Dan Quayle in this format. Criticism of this format is that it limits the topics discussed, and it allows the candidates to rely on prerehearsed answers. However, it does provide for a highly focused program, one where reporters have an opportunity to press candidates to answer questions that a candidate might prefer not to answer.

Another format is the mini-debate. Such an event might be as short as 1 minute, or as long as 7 minutes. It would fit within a news broadcast. This format is not advisable in a large field unless all the eligible candidates can participate at one time.

Debate sponsorship is a topic of continuing discussion. The problem for the broadcaster is to ensure that any debate is sponsored by a group that will provide a program that is both balanced and suitable and can keep the interest of an electronic-media audience. Many broadcasters believe that if they sponsor the debate, they can determine a format that provides the most interesting program for electronic media. The League of Women Voters, on the other hand, says that independent sponsorship is important if third-party candidates are ever to get equal time. Another option is the debate sponsored by candidates themselves, using satellite technology. In developing a campaign plan, broadcasters might find it useful to incorporate all of these variations. To do so would allow the audience to hear the candidate in different situations: one structured to be a good media program; one structured to emphasize longer dialogue on an issue; and another structured to let the candidate's campaign determine the message.

The interest of the broadcaster to inform the electorate through a debate may not always be consistent with the interests of candidates. Lee Atwater, prominent Republican campaign advisor, argued that in 1984, while presidential debates are probably unavoidable, it was not in Ronald Reagan's interest to debate. "Why take the risk if the numbers show you are ahead?"[27] In the past, debates have been cancelled when one participant declines to participate. However, support is growing for the policy of broadcasting the event with an empty chair. The empty-chair policy enables the voter to see that someone chose not to communicate with the public. To cancel the debate does not inform the public of the candidate's strategy to avoid public contact.

Special Coverage Formats
Political coverage formats are limited only by broadcasters' imaginations. Here are some frequently used approaches.

Designated Free Time   One variation on the special coverage format is to provide free time equally to all the candidates for a given office. In the United States 19.5% of the stations surveyed offered free time to candidates in 1986; 10.9% of these offers were the result of candidates requesting time longer than that allocated for commercials. Of the stations surveyed, 18.2% made deliberate decisions not to provide free time. But 63.4% got no request from candidates. If provided, free time might be simply time for a lengthy commercial, or it might provide coverage of a candidate speech, or it may be a block of time designated for a candidate to use as the campaign deems appropriate.

In 1982, the Federal Election Commission (FEC) ruled that it did not violate the Federal Election Campaign Act ban on political contributions by corporations for broadcasters to offer free air time to political parties if it is offered equally.[28] Free coverage solves the problem of a campaign not being able to communicate its message directly to the voter. It also serves to ensure coverage for those candidates who are not wealthy enough to buy extensive advertising. For the broadcaster, 3- to 5-minute segments of free time to all candidates for a race could be fit comfortably into the regular broadcast schedule within the last week before the elections. It may, in fact, provide a better public service for less total broadcast time and less production cost than preparing station-sponsored comprehensive half-hour or hour election shows that either emphasize commentary or lose audience because they become boring.

Talk Shows   Another special program technique that solves the problem of voter access to the candidates might be to follow the lead of KCRW in California in offering a series of talks with candidates for President. Their programs featured a half-hour of direct listener questions to the candidate.[29] In Sweden, a radio station provided a follow-up "call in" for listeners after a television station carried a major candidate program. Talk shows can provide the voter an opportunity to ask questions directly of the candidate, making the voter an active part of the electoral process. From the broadcaster's viewpoint, political talk shows on selected occasions can generate audience interest in the station, beyond that of the station's usual demographics. Don't allow political talk shows to last so long that they cut into the normal broadcast pattern of the station. In an election, the occasional talk show, even if calls are prescreened to guarantee a full range of pertinent topics, is preferable to "spin doctors"—self-proclaimed political forecasters—making post-debate commentary.

Features   Features are another special coverage format. Such programs will be an advantage for the station interested in attracting a new news audience. They might even help in news ratings. Special programs will certainly attract a "political junkie" audience—people who think it's high theater. In addition, if the personalities, issues, or elections are controversial, the audience will expand. People are still fascinated with politicians, bankers, and developers, even if they sometimes hate them.[30]

The content of such features can vary greatly. One could analyze the campaign strategies used by different candidates and discuss them in terms of the demographics of the district. One might focus on campaign finances looking at whose money buys what favors and products. A human-interest program on each candidate's personal background might enable the voter to understand the culture and values that the candidate is likely to represent. Another possibility would be to focus on the voter's view of the office to which someone will be elected. What's the job of that office? Does it really benefit the taxpayer? For example, what does the mayor's office really do? Opportunity exists for using "infotainment" and drama to convey information in feature programs.

GOTV—GETTING OUT THE VOTE

Surveys by NAB have concluded that the industry has certainly done its share to "get out the vote." In 1988, 84.4% of radio stations and 63.3% of TV stations planned local newscast stories encouraging voter participation in elections. In addition, public service directors at 94% of radio stations and 89.2% of television stations planned Public Service Announcements (PSA) to encourage voting.[31]

The National Association of Broadcasters is proud of the work it does on behalf of broadcasters in concert with other concerned groups, for example, the Vote America campaign. The association is a clearinghouse for spots, scripts, and produced PSAs, and sends these out nationally; the local station can add its own tag line. Local broadcasters add their own imagination to the effort and sponsor a range of local activities that encourage voters to participate. One must not forget, however, that getting out the vote is encouraged not only by the public service campaign, but also by how the ongoing election coverage is handled. The broadcaster has a unique challenge to personalize the events of the election enough so that the viewer/listener shifts gears from passive to active. That will not only strengthen democratic systems of government, it will also result in more enthusiasm for programs, higher ratings, and greater revenues.

CONCLUSION

Journalism is a portrait of reality on which a citizen can act.
—Walter Lippmann [32]

Election coverage offers exciting new avenues to involve the growing news audience in programming that is exciting, entertaining, real competition, and an avenue for fulfilling the expectations of the framers of the Constitution, who designated for the press a role given no other private entity. "It is incumbent. . . upon the profession in general, not just television journalists, to become more sensitized to the changing nature of the 'game' and develop new rules that would nurture the creation of new news source strategies, accuracy tests, and balance, especially in these hotly contested situations where the 'truth' has so many potential faces."[33]

Notes

1. Personal interview with Dr. Richard Ducey, Director of Research and Planning, National Association of Broadcasters, Washington, D. C., February 14, 1990.
2. Personal interview with Andrea Mitchell, Chief Congressional Correspondent, NBC Television, February 14, 1990.
3. The author participated as a member of 20-member Platform Drafting Committee for National Convention in 1984.
4. Timothy J. Russert, "For '92, Networks Have to Do Better," *New York Times*, March 4, 1990, p. E23.
5. WCVB-TV, Boston, videotape submission for the Edward R. Murrow Award for Continuing Coverage in 1988.
6. Personal interview with Emily Rooney, WCVB-TV News Director (formerly 1988 Campaign Director of WCVB-TV Political Unit), March 5, 1990.
7. Ibid.
8. Phil Balboni was WCVB-TV News Director at the time of developing the 1988 plan and deserves recognition for his work.
9. WCVB-TV, Murrow submission.

10. "Fall Radio Winners: News and Urban Contemporary," *Broadcasting*, January 8, 1990, p. 58.

11. Personal interview, Chuck Crouse, WEEI-Boston reporter who traveled with the Presidential campaign in 1988 and covers state and local political issues, January 30, 1990.

12. Charles Kravetz, 1990 Political Director, "Memorandum," WCVB-TV, Boston, February 13, 1990.

13. Ibid.

14. Arthur Nielsen, "Television Ratings," in Jon T. and Wally Gair, eds., *Public Interest and the Business of Broadcasting: The Broadcast Industry Looks at Itself* (New York: Quorum Books, 1988), 62.

15. "Network Television Audiences to: Primaries, Conventions and Elections," 1987 Update Edition Nielsen Television Index, Nielsen Media Research, New York.

16. Personal interview with Adrienne Lotoski, Director of Research, WCVB-TV, Boston (former represenrative of Arbitron Ratings Company), May 1, 1990.

17. Interview with Ducey.

18. Data furnished from 1988 National Association of Broadcasters' reports provided to the author. Ibid.

19. W.C. Adams, *Television Coverage of the 1980 Presidential Election Campaign* (Norwood, N.J. Abley, 1983), 134.

20. Bill Moyers, "The Public Mind," WGBH-TV, Boston, November 22, 1989.

21. Personal interview with Jim Quello, FCC Commissioner, Washington, D.C., February 16, 1990.

22. Melvin Mencher, *Basic News Writing*, 3d. ed. (Dubuque, Iowa: W.C. Brown, 1989), 52.

23. Austin Ranney, *Channels of Power: The Impact of Television on American Politics* (New York: Basic Books, 1983), 67–68.

24. "Six O'Clock News," WCVB-TV Boston, March 6, 1990.

25. Joel L. Swerdlow, ed., *Media Technology and the Vote: A Source Book* (Washington, D.C.: Annenberg Washington Program, 1988), 77.

26. "Political Airtime '86" (summary of a survey of television-station results conducted for NAB by National Research, Inc.) Washington, D.C.: National Association of Broadcasters, 1986.

27. "Campaigning on Cue" videotape produced by WTTW, Chicago, after the 1984 elections.

28. "FEC Lets Broadcasters Offer the Two Parties Free Time," *Washington Post*, August 27, 1982, p. A19: "Free Air Time Offer Is Upheld," *New York Times*, August 27, 1982.

29. Steve Weinstein, "KCRW Links Listeners to Candidates," *Los Angeles Times*, October 16, 1987, pt. VI, p. 28.

30. Personal interview with Dan Payne, political media consultant, Boston, February 6, 1990.

31. "Broadcasters Help to Get Out the Vote," National Association of Broadcasters Press Release #58/88, Washington, D.C., 1988.

32. Moyers, "The Public Mind."

33. Paraschos,"Abstract: Network Coverage of the 1988 Bush Ambush of Boston."

3

▼ Reporters and Election
▼ Coverage

ELECTRONIC ELECTIONS
AND ENIGMATIC ELOQUENCE

Jesse Jackson captured the essence of electronic media election reporting when he observed that if one is ungrammatic, it's ignorance, and if one is grammatic, it's boring. So, being enigmatic is a media hallmark for candidates.

Over the centuries communication has taken many forms. Today, the approach must differ from that applied to print media, just as print approaches differed from the oratory of ancient Greek democracies. Candidates and reporters both must adapt to new formats that enable successful communication via electronic media. Language must be charismatic and quotable. Jesse Jackson received good media coverage when he said, "Demonstrate, don't hesitate. Be willing to go to jail, without bail." How much media coverage would be given to the statement, "I think it is important to make our position clear even if it means breaking the law to right a social wrong."[1]

For reporters, newswriters, and newscasters, mastering the equipment and the writing techniques required for electronic broadcasting is just the first step. Mastering election coverage requires added techniques, sensitivity and imagination. What is different about approaching the who, what, where, when, and how of election coverage?

REPORTING ELECTIONS

The Overall Framework

Ideally, appropriate persons within the station will develop an election plan for the station as discussed in Chapter 2. The station plays an important role in the elections, whether at a local or national level. Robert MacNeil of PBS suggested the role for a national network at a Fordham University conference: "I don't think television sets the agenda as much as it dramatizes it, and therefore sets it in people's heads."[2]

Stations do determine who and what gets covered. They decide the extent of the coverage. They decide the tone of the coverage. The job for reporters is not easy. Covering elections is like covering a panel of blind persons describing an elephant. There is no single authoritative view of what's happening in an election.

▲ 28

Know the Subject

Reporters learn journalism and broadcasting techniques, but do they also understand political science? Seldom is there time to focus on knowing more than one subject well. It is important to take the time to think about what you're covering—the forest, not the trees. Only then will you be able to do a top-notch job.

Measure the candidates against the job description for the position available, just as you would measure an athlete against the records set for the sport. Know the jurisdiction for the office and how it works (see Chapter 8). Systems work differently in different parts of the country, and the locality where your station is may function quite differently from the locality where your home is. Laws vary. Practices vary and the same entity may have different names. Sometimes a "secretary" is the person who types and files and sometimes the "secretary" is the person who decides and directs. Sometimes local judges are elected, sometimes appointed. Some communities have a single property tax, others may either have separate taxes for separate public products or they may be assessed by county rather than by municipality. Some places have counties. In other places, counties don't count, as in New England, for example. Learn how to research and where to find the information necessary for award winning coverage.

The Reporter's Assignment

Covering elections is a natural extension of a reporter's ongoing job. Be a reader. Read everything that comes across your desk. Learn about issues. Be a generalist who is willing to specialize. Go to background briefings. Talk to "think tanks." Talk to people even if it seems peripheral and doesn't produce a story that day. A broadcaster needs to be a vacuum cleaner.[3]

Be a good writer. Write with clarity. The best way to lose credibility quickly is to be an imprecise writer. In a network, for example, the New York producers will see your written script before it is approved for airing. You can get thrown to the wolves quickly and be written off before you get started.

Andrea Mitchell, NBC Chief Congressional Correspondent in Washington, began her career in a local station in Philadelphia. "To work in a network or a station, one must see oneself as part of a team," she said. "I've learned a great deal from camera people who see a lot through their lens, and then, from the tape editor who is trained to see with yet another perspective. Everyone contributes something."[4]

Apply as many generic skills as you have to covering the candidates, their campaigns, and the voters making decisions about the future direction of their district. As you examine the election coverage suggestions below, you will need to think about how you can fit new ideas for election coverage within the basic structure of reporting for your medium.

Radio   If you work for radio you may have many tasks. Perhaps only a couple of hundred radio street reporters exist in the entire country. More common is the person who spends part of the day doing newscasts and part of it reporting, such as making the rounds of key government offices. The average station has 1½ to 2½ newspeople and is basically interested in music. In fact, it may offer no news broadcasts evenings and weekends.

How elections are covered depends on the views of the general manager and the credibility of the news director. Some stations historically cover elections simply by going to City Hall the night the votes are counted. More can be done, even if the station is short-staffed. For example, if a reporter can operate within a prescribed campaign plan, more coverage can be provided with less reporter time.

A news reporter is a luxury for a radio station in terms of air time filled—compared to the disc jockey whose records account for many hours of air time. But the reporter is able to bring the station some special qualities valued by listeners—immediacy, accuracy, and credibility.[5] Chuck Crouse, veteran radio reporter and columnist for the Radio and Television News Directors Association, (RTNDA) says:

> The reporter exists to gather news directly: to be the eyes and ears of the station, and of its listeners. A lot of news can be covered from the desk, mostly by telephone, but that often amounts to second-hand coverage. Since news happens outside the station, it takes someone in the field to cover it first hand: to catch the sounds, the feel, and the nuances of what transpires.[6]

Remember, the radio audience is likely doing something else while listening, so the reporter must capture the listener's attention quickly and then concisely tell the chronology of the story. This must be done in a way that informs through creating images. A story might run 60 seconds—that is 15 lines of copy at 65 characters per line, or it could be only 20 or 30 seconds. Selection criterion must focus on controversial, interesting, attention getting items.[7]

If the reporter works within the framework of a campaign coverage plan, as suggested in Chapter 2, effective election news can be broadcast regularly. Data and file tape can be readily available to supplement daily activity. In addition, coverage can be enhanced if radio, television, and newspapers can complement each other's coverage and collaborate on data bank development.

Television   If you work for a television station, you understand that TV reporting does not describe events. It shows them. It minimizes telling about things. It lets them happen.[8] It is critical to television news to open with a lead that instantly telegraphs the story, show compelling visual action, keep it simple, and end with a strong closing, proving everything visually. The four basic components to TV news gathering are:

1. Visual image
2. Sound
3. Tape editing for sequence, length, juxtaposition
4. Words—just enough to bridge visuals lightly and to coordinate.[9]

While adapting to this technology has produced "sound-bites" and the visual equivalent, "photo ops," it is time to emphasize the opportunities this technology offers for more responsible election coverage. Too much attention has been focused on the negative.

Television allows voters to "entertain" the candidates in their own living rooms, to get some sense of the people running. Television brings even the most apolitical individual some exposure to the fact of the election and the choices available. More Americans have at least a passing acquaintance with the details of campaigns than was the case before television. But television has yet to reach its potential. Appropriate and substantive election coverage is still at the experimental stage. The data available to stations to analyze "what works" and "what doesn't work" is still sparse. National elections give us the best common database for evaluating uses of the new technologies for election coverage. We have had only eight national elections since the medium was first used in 1960, with the use of campaign media and polling consultants growing in the 1970s and technological advances proliferating in the 1980s. The kind of planning discussed in Chapter 3 is very new. The exciting work ahead is for broadcasters to learn from the experience of the past and to apply the strengths of this technology to future election coverage at every level of government.

BREAK THE STORY! BURN THE SOURCE?

The media's independence is the main beam of democracy. In politics, especially, reporters frequently rely on personal sources, although their validity needs to be documented, if possible, with sound research as discussed in Chapter 8.

Personal sources provide both a "breakthrough" and a "bondage" for the reporter. A "break story versus burn source" tension develops that, in its worst manifestation, results in a compromised and dependent press. A reporter can't get caught in the trap of refusing to break a story because of the value of keeping sources, observes Andrea Mitchell. A young reporter will lose her independence. Remember, breaking a story earns respect. Be careful about being circuitous and getting information through social contacts. Candidates and officials know that it is a reporters job to get information and they know it is a somewhat adversarial relationship. Be careful about accepting "off the record deep background information." It can be just another way of co-opting the press. Background information is useful, but a reporter must use judgment about the extent of the nonattributable material provided.

When a reporter breaks a story, even if it's controversial, one earns respect from colleagues and sometimes from enemies. Sometimes one gets burned. But it is usually possible to get around the problem. A good reporter develops many sources at all levels—horizontally as well as vertically—and can find someone else who was consulted or someone who dislikes the person who won't talk. Actually, says Mitchell, "the most fun is breaking a story—working the phones, checking and double checking until you know you've got it, then releasing it." Mitchell was the first reporter to break the story that George Bush would choose Dan Quayle to be Vice-President.[10]

TRAPS TO AVOID

The tone of coverage determines the quality of coverage as much as does the substance of the story or the format of the program. These intangibles reflect the conscious, or unconscious, biases or cultural orientation or expediency of the individuals associated with decisions of what is covered at every level. For high-quality election coverage, scrutinize your reporting to be sure you don't fall into any of the following traps.

The Passive Press

"So pervasive is the passivity of the press that when a reporter actually looks for news on his or her own it is given a special name, 'investigative journalism,' to distinguish it from routine passive 'source journalism.'"[11] The problem of passivity is discussed more and more. Several factors contribute to it. Fear that management won't support investigative journalism contributes to conformity and passivity. In addition, we all find it easier to take the level path rather than one over the hill. Schedules are full. Deadlines are too close. Sometimes just getting the job done is a major accomplishment. Accepting a tape in ready-to-air form from a campaign saves work. That extra measure of effort to do the award-winning investigative journalism piece may require more effort than one can exert.

Sometimes the passivity of the press is called "objectivity."[12] The idea pervades that nothing can be said unless an "official" spokesperson says it. Rationalization of this sort is easy when pressures are great. It is also true that unless one has planned ahead, access to credible information and spokespersons to offer the other side of a story may take too long. The solution? Factor the consideration into development of the station's plan for election coverage.

When media do not exhibit some "chutzpa" about their independent role, they can get led by candidates. Be careful of the images offered by the candidates. For example, the George Bush 1988 campaign focused excessively on "flag factory" images, that is, the perception that candidate Bush's campaign emphasized patriotism, visiting flag factories, figuratively wrapping himself in the American flag, and largely ignoring issues. This is an approach frequently used by candidates. Such images have relatively little to do with the credentials and skills of the candidate. The media must learn to discern what is happening.

Tarmac Journalism

Tarmac journalism reflects the propensity for "gang-bang" press conferences and "photo ops" taken at various airports for national and state-wide elections. At a local level, one might consider the candidate-convened press conference a similar event. For overworked reporters this sometimes seems the best way to get the most information. And it may be cheaper than sending crews out to get new footage in less central locations.

The anecdote told by Boston's WEEI News Radio's Chuck Crouse in his February 8 and 9, 1987, "Reporter's Journal" illustrates the "herd" mentality of tarmac journalism: "Several local [Iowa] reporters told the traveling Boston press that they hadn't been planning to cover Dukakis, until they learned that there was this army of reporters coming with him. So the herd instinct thrives in Iowa newsrooms, as in Washington or Boston."

In principle, following another reporter's tip is a fine idea, just as long as it doesn't become a substitute for thorough reporting. A well developed station campaign plan will help keep balanced election coverage, while leaving room for the flexibility needed to cover new developments not anticipated when the plan was developed.

Out of Context

Dealing with the immediate can sometimes become so all-encompassing that it is hard to remember that everything has a context. For example, when the press reported that "George Bush declared in his Republican convention acceptance speech, 'I will ban chemical and biological weapons from the face of the earth,' not one TV correspondent or anchorperson at the convention mentioned that Bush's tie-breaking votes in the Senate in 1983 allowed a renewal and escalation of U.S. chemical weapons production, and in 1986 Bush cast a tie-breaking vote that allowed the development of the Big Eye (nerve gas) bomb."[13]

Different reporters may have covered the earlier stories, and those covering the convention may never have known about the earlier record. But they should have. The solution? Access to a computer file on each vote and each candidate that can be automatically retrieved when candidates address a given issue. Develop a databank that includes candidate positions, voting records, and prior activity.

Sometimes Less Is More

A biased "spin" (commentary) on a story may make for colorful reporting, but if you remember that covering elections differs from covering regular news, you'll want the audience to be able to make their own judgment on the candidates. Chuck Crouse also observed that "reporters are no more cheerleaders than they are prosecutors."[14] Reporters have different backgrounds and experiences. Personal reaction must be separated from the fair account. Resist the temptation to use phrases that bias the listener/viewer.

Only the voters have the right to decide on the candidates. It is not appropriate to report, as the press frequently does, that the field is "unimpressive,"[15] or for the media to make the value judgment that 1988 Democratic presidential candidate, Illinois Senator Paul Simon "must be second in New Hampshire to survive." Reports such as these undermine the right of millions of voters to decide for themselves on Election Day. How can one rationally say that 3,442 votes in New Hampshire will preempt the right of 180 million Americans to make their choice?[16]

Another example of excessive commentary is the "spin" on debates that generally concludes that the best "one-liner" wins the debate. The one-liner may have added entertainment to the evening. It may have gotten a clever candidate a few more minutes of media time. But it certainly should not be the determining factor in one's ability to govern effectively, nor should it preempt the voters' right to make their choice. Democracy differs from the Academy Awards.

"They are candidates for causes" is another media evaluation. This unspecified negative easily dismisses candidates who may be very thoughtful individuals with substance to bring to the campaign and to the future direction for the school district, or the state, or the nation. This generalized categorizing can contribute to the problem identified by many students of American politics: "Government is being crippled by a new superstructure of politics that makes ideas harder to discuss and exalts public opinion over leadership."[17]

Too much commentary is inappropriate in election coverage. The solution? Give the listener/viewer an accurate portrayal of what happened with enough analysis to see the events in context. Make no judgments. Draw no conclusions. That is up to the voter.

Inadvertent Sex and Race Bias

Discrimination tends to be subtle these days, but perhaps even more damaging than when the enemy was visible. The traps are in the use of language, assumption, and "ghetto-ization". The minority or female candidate spends considerable energy just fighting for the right to play on the team—the right to be present so one can be assessed by one's capabilities.

An analysis of 3,215 stories on print and broadcast journalism in the Boston media market in 1986 shows that only white "experts" are quoted when discussing black community concerns. It further documents that the average black citizen is seldom covered, but that the media concentrates on celebrities—from show business to athletes to criminals. Of the coverage about the black community 85% reinforces stereotypes by playing on issues involving drugs, crime, poverty, and apathy. This coverage undercuts esteem in the black community and reinforces white stereotypes.[18] How, in this environment, can a black candidate emerge as a person of stature able to address the full range of issues required by a mayor or a governor?

Minorities compose 23½% of the U.S. population (8½% Hispanic, 12% Black, 3% Asian). Yet, in 1990 only 4 ¼% of federal elected officials are minority (0 in the executive branch, 0 of 100 in the Senate, and 23 of 435 in the House of Representatives). At state and local levels the figures are not much better. Only 1 of 50 Governors is black. Of thousands of municipalities in the country, only 301 had black Mayors.[19] Hispanic representation is even worse despite the considerable Hispanic population in a number of southern and western states. Of this nation's 504,404 elected officials, 3,783, or less than 1%, are Hispanic.[20]

Women, while 52% of the population in the United States, have far less than an equal share of elected office holders. In 1989, 4 ⅔% of the federal elected officials were women (0 in the executive branch, 2 of 100 in the Senate, and 23 of 435 in the House of Representatives). At a state level it is not much better—15%. Included in this figure are five women Governors. Women represent 14% of local elected officials.[21] "What is most striking . . . is the contrast between the large numbers of women active in grass roots politics and the negligible number who win election to public office of any sort."[22]

The discrimination of perception creates a reality for women. "Women candidates lose because they don't have enough money to conduct effective campaigns; they have trouble raising money because people think they're losers; and round and round it goes."[23]

Stereotyping, a quick commentary, or a bias that underlies the story remain obstacles for minority and women candidates. Pat Fullinwider was a candidate for Congress from Arizona who noted that when she talked about tax reforms, closing loopholes, and cutting $107 billion, the press wanted to know her source, a question they would not ask a white male candidate.[24] This happens even though the minority or the woman, (as in the case of Lt. Governor Evelyn Murphy, a candidate in 1990 for Governor of Massachusetts) has a Ph.D. in economics and more years experience in the field than her male opponents. The subtle assumption is that the white male is probably more of an expert.

Jeane Kirkpatrick, not known as a feminist, addresses the subtlety of sexism: "Part of the women's problem is the male's unawareness of both his privilege and his tendency, if not conspiracy, to resist sharing power with women."[25]

Fighting to get into the ballpark ought to have been left behind with the Civil War. For a representative democracy to work, those who report on elections must not be trapped by myth. They must not assume that "experts" are white males only. Similarly, they must not assume that minorities care only about stereotypical minority issues. Reporters must not assume that white men should be spared the questions about racial equality, children, and health care and ask these questions principally of minority and female candidates. The energies of all candidates must be focused on the main agenda items of the campaign, not in fighting brushfires of media bigotry.

The solution? Test what is said for bigotry by seeing how the same thing sounds when said about a candidate of a different sex or race. For example, if you're tempted to introduce the female candidate for attorney general as "an environmental activist" despite her current position as Assistant Attorney General, see how it would sound to you to introduce her male counterpart that way—by categorizing rather than by position—and ignoring the stature appropriate for a top-level official. The media do this frequently.

Symbols and Images

Symbols and images are magnified by television. In the absence of thoughtful reporting, they can distort the reality of a situation. With thoughtful reporting, they can add impact to a story. For example, U.S. Senator Mike Gravel of Alaska spearheaded the 1973 drive to build the Alaska Pipeline, carefully balancing interests in preserving Alaska's environment with improving both the state and national economy. At the time of an energy crisis, considerable benefit was derived from making it possible for 20% of America's oil supply to come from domestic sources, and improving the nation's balance of payments by $170 billion. A humorous photo shows him straddling the pipeline, delighted with the significant documents in his hand. Out of context, that image could distort the importance of his role and the widespread public support for his approach. The image could, effectively, lie.[26]

Symbols are critical to television and to elections. Throughout history, symbols have been used to identify those associated with a point of view, from the Star of David to the swastika. Symbols embodying a person's image or interest must be selected carefully, for no individual should be reduced to a "snapshot" image. What is needed is to choose images used for a particular story only after taking a hard look at what the candidate stands for and what the candidate's skills are, even if that candidate is not your personal choice. Change the image of the candidate, as appropriate, for other stories.

Glamour   The anesthesia of glamour sometimes misleads us into confusing statespersons and stars. Performers, the so-called beautiful people, become the most successful candidates regardless of their credentials.[27] Reporters must not fall into that trap, and they must guard against leading their listeners/viewers in that direction. Admittedly, glamour does bring a rise in the number of listeners or viewers. But there are ways to use this technique with harmless humor that does not discriminate against any candidate. The following example was in a radio broadcast: *"Playgirl magazine lists Dukakis on its ten sexiest men list—with actor Tom Cruise, Michael Jordan of the Chicago Bulls, smut jock Howard Stern, and Rupert Murdoch."*[28]

Gold   Those who are the wealthiest candidates, or those able to raise the most money from either wealthy constituents or from political action committees (PACs), with strings attached, are by and large the most successful candidates. Democratic Congressperson David Obey of Wisconsin states, "One test of viability—would be whether money could be raised, and that's determined pretty much by whether you can show up in the polls at all, and that, in turn, is determined in large part by whether you can get any visibility at all on television."[29]

The problem is that the wealthiest candidate may not be the best qualified candidate. Reporters must not allow themselves to fall into the trap of assessing early viability by wealth. The practice automatically handicaps all candidates who might represent another segment of the population. The solution is to design a station campaign coverage plan that builds in coverage opportunities for all candidates and to follow the plan.

Labels   Missouri Democrat Jean Berg ran for Congress in 1976. Despite the fact that professionally she was a hospital services administrator, the media depicted her as a housewife zealous about social causes.[30] Subtle but effective discrimination is the use of labels for those one does not traditionally think of as having a title. Minorities and women candidates frequently report this problem. Despite her title as an elected Democratic National Committeewoman, and her professional position directing a respected program at an area university, Betty Taymore of Massachusetts never was able to sensitize senior Massachusetts officials to introduce her as someone other than "the mother of those three beautiful children." Most of the women, Hispanics, and blacks running for office have professional and political titles. Don't fall into the trap of referring to them as "activists." Reporters might make it their policy to refer to all candidates in a common manner. Always use titles—elected office, appointed office, or job title. Labels are subjective descriptions imposed by outsiders. Titles are indicative of a candidate's actual credentials.

Cynicism

Thomas Patterson, professor of political science at Syracuse's Maxwell School, has noted that the "tone and content of news coverage of politics has darkened dramatically over the last 30 years."[31] Reporters need to be reminded that there are many people who come to government at considerable sacrifice and for reasons that are very high-minded. *Bureaucrat* is not a dirty word. Some people have an almost academic approach to their professions. They hope to contribute. There are elected officials at every level of government who have not accumulated power by heavy-handed means. They are highly respected for their contribution to the public well-being. Don't become too jaded and too cynical. Keep an open mind.

Theology of Polling

Chapter 6 focuses on the opportunities and the distortions that come from relying on polling data. Don't become such a true believer that you fail to discern the subtleties of the data. Don't get locked in a time warp viewing a September primary election as a still photograph taken in March polling. Another photo taken in the same location in the November general election (or maybe only a few days after the first poll) might look very different. Elections and the views of society are organic. Things change constantly. It would be a shame if they didn't. Civilization would make no progress and the daily news would be too boring to bother about. Polling is graffiti; don't portray it as granite. The chapter on polling provides suggestions on effective use of polls.

TECHNIQUES FOR ELECTION REPORTING

A number of techniques can be helpful to reporters covering elections.

Identify Candidate Selection Time

Begin election coverage early. While underemphasized by the public and the media, during those weeks and months long before election day critical decisions are made about who one can choose. This is the ideal time for computer-graphic stories listing the job description for the positions to be elected in your market, advance "calendar" postings for the benchmark deadlines for certifying as a legally qualified candidate, a sportscaster approach to measuring early candidate specific records against the job requirements, or perhaps features on how past decisions by the given office have affected the lives of typical district residents. Remember, one problem the public has with politics is a sense that it is remote from the day-to-day concerns of typical people. Candidate selection time is an ideal period for bringing the topic "home" and developing an audience interested in participating as the whole drama unfolds.

Media Collaboration

Consider collaborative ventures among television, radio, and newspapers. Promote each for what it does best. Television might get the public's attention with visuals chosen to illustrate what's happening and why it matters. Radio might reinforce this and provide talk show opportunities to discuss the subtleties. Print media might follow up with appropriate in-depth analysis. Explore the possibilities for news stories and calendar announcements in your market, and new, mutually beneficial opportunities for media collaboration. One example of collaboration is that of WEEI radio in Boston and a local newspaper, *The Boston Globe,* jointly contracting with the Gallup polling organization for polling data. Local employees would read the results and analysis, and the station and the newspaper would decide who would break which part of the news when. Television prefers to break stories in the evening whereas radio and newspapers find morning news releases more appropriate.

NAT SOT FULL Rostenkowski walking into hall	"Boo...Boo...Chicken" When loyal Democrats turn on Dan Rostenkowski. . . the popular Chairman of the House Ways and Means Committee. . . .Con gress knows it's in trouble.
SOT Jean Gray (woman inside)	"We're not going to vote for him in the next elec tion. We're very very angry with him because he won't even listen to the people."
VOICE-OVER...people pounding on the car roof outside	Across the country. . . Angry senior citizens are protesting the added cost of catastrophic health care.
NAT SOT people	"Down with Rosty" "Coward" And they wouldn't let him get away:
SOT FULL Dan Rostenkowski	"They don't understand what the government is trying to do for them"
ESS...Pamphlets, advertisements EJ...Mailroom at National Committee to Save Social Security and Medicare	The elderly have been whipped into action by advertising from powerful lobbying groups. The result: millions of letters and care postcards to Congress.
VOICE-OVER elderly patients in Miami nursing home	They're not against the new benefits: Unlimited hospital care. . . new at-home benefits . . . prescription drug coverage. They just don't want to pay for them.
SOT Harold Dorf (man in Miami nursing home)	"We wanted the benefits, but we didn't want those who could afford to, to pay for all those who the government should pay for"
ESS...Chyron Payment Plan	All people enrolled in medicare pay four dollars more a month for catastrophic coverage. What is angering the elderly is an additional surtax paid on a sliding scale by higher-income people. Those with incomes of 35-thousand dollars a year pay the maximum surtax: 800 dollars a year. Only 1.6 million people. . . 5 percent of all Medi-care receiptents. . . would pay the maximum. But they are the best organized...and the most vocal.

▶ *Figure 4   Participation molds policy. Reprinted courtesy of Andrea Mitchell, Chief Congressional Correspondent, NBC News, Washington, D.C.*

NAT SOT FULL	NAT SOT FULL
SOT Ken Hoagland National Committee to Preserve Social Security and Medicare	"Asking seniors to pay the full cost of this program is not fair, it is not equitable. We don't ask other age segments to do that."
VOICE-OVER factory workers	In fact. . . all workers subsidize medicare benefits through their social security taxes.
Old folks in Miami	But that has not made it any easier to persuade the elderly to pay for new benefits.
STANDUP CLOSE	Congress is considering a plan to cut the surtax in half. . . and shift the costs to all medicare receipients, not just those with higher incomes/ critics say that would be even worse.
	The mood is getting so bad. . . many congress men want to get rid of the whole program...and silence the critics.
	Andrea Mitchell, NBC News, Washington.

▶ *Figure 4* (continued)

Activate the Audience

Reporters have many options for activating the audience. A compelling script can do it. The script deals with the issue of catastrophic health care insurance. It does not treat the issue in a vacuum—as if it were a policy created by no one. Rather, it connects the policy to the policy-makers to the electoral process—a practical reminder to the viewer/voter of how the process of self-government works.

Other options exist for activating the audience. Report to listeners how, when, and where they can have input to the process. For example, the following public servicement announcement:

1. "Your party caucus to elect the delegates who chose the candidates at the state convention will be held ————. Call ———— if you want to go."
2. "At present ———— candidates have registered with the Election Commission. Here are the names and telephone numbers of each campaign so you can learn more or go to their headquarters."
3. "Next Tuesday, March 11th at 5:45 P.M. the issue of———— will be dis cussed in one of our 25 issue pieces. Your elected ———— will determine ———— (example of how the issue affects a typical citizen). After the program, exercise your right to send a postcard to the candidates telling them how this issue affects you. Here's the addresses."

Activating the viewers/listeners also happens in subtle ways throughout the entire election season, culminating in the election night. Each story aired is written with care not to provide so much commentary that the voters' right to make the decision is preempted. In fact, as election day approaches, stories can be written that remind voter that the decision is theirs.

In years ahead, creative broadcasters will find ways to use the new technologies that allow for instant voter response (see Chapter 7). Such technology can be more "personal" than polling, involve whomever is interested, connect more directly with news events, and be used to validate the importance of the individual's view without preempting the actual election.

Involve All the Candidates

Just as in a sports event, all the official entries deserve equal coverage until the voters—not the reporters—decide who is out of the running. Be fair. Give everyone an equal chance. Never, never use the phrase "and also running."

Andrea Mitchell speaks as a voter in the District of Columbia and describes the problem: "If I were here as a local reporter in the District of Columbia with a Mayor's race coming up I'd be out there letting people know a whole lot more about these candidates. I'm a fairly interested political observer. I live in D.C. The only potential candidates I hear about are Jesse Jackson, a national figure; the travails of Marion Barry, the incumbent, and occasionally Walter Fauntroy, the District of Columbia's appointee to the U.S. Congress. No one covers those on the City Council who might run. One of them might be a good candidate. Also, it may be easier to engage people in improving government at local level. At a national level, so many people feel shut out."[32]

A number of excuses are offered for not providing full and fair coverage. High on the list is the theory that as long as the broadcast systems are privately operated they need to show a profit and that requires maintaining an audience. Once an early generalized osmotic decision is made regarding who is not likely to win, those candidates don't get coverage. It is unfair to the candidates and to the public. But time is limited and management does not want to cover anything that might not attract an audience. If people don't like a song, the station doesn't play it. Playing up frontrunners in a horserace is safer.[33]

It is innaccurate to apply the same editorial standards for radio music or television sitcoms to election coverage. The audience constantly listens to news items that it doesn't necessarily like. It listens because it might affect them personally. Fair election coverage means covering all the options because every option might effect the quality of life of the audience. Fair coverage can be accomplished without boring or alienating the audience. Candidates who are not "stars" need not be boring. Whether or not a program is boring depends on the format, how the content is developed, how material is edited, and what visuals are selected. The reporter controls the momentum. Good script writing, action visuals, and effective use of computer graphics can be used to draw out the opportunities that exist in every campaign. By spending some time with the candidate and her staff, a good reporter can identify potential stories within that campaign.

Another reason for eclipsing some candidates is that in a crowded field it is logistically easier. It takes less time to cover and mention only some of the names, and to allow reporters or pollsters to designate "frontrunners" and "second tier" candidates. It is possible, however, for the conscientious reporter not to preempt the voter. For example:

1. Don't say the names of three candidates in the field followed by "and also several others." Say the names of all the legally qualified candidates.
2. If taping a debate of 11 candidates, instruct the camera person and the editor to be sure that at least one shot of 3 or 4 seconds pans *each* candidate's face *and* name plate.
3. If a news story features 2 or 3 of the 11 be sure that comparable time is allocated for all the others. Comparable time means time of day, day of week, number of weeks before actual election, and comparable substance. And don't pair candidates in "tiers"—mix them up.
4. Never sponsor "tiered" debates. Ideally, have all 11 on air at the same time, even if this means they only answer one question each. If air time makes that unwieldy, announce that the two or three groups are paired in debates by having drawn lots.

Pull the Curtain Mystifying Campaign Strategy

Informing the electorate about elections requires shining the spotlight on the strategy of winning elections. For example, a story could be written on the number of voters needed to win in a given district, who is likely to cast a vote, and how each campaign is targeting its message to the part of the constituency important to a given candidate. Another story could be written about issues important to people in the district, what each of the candidates have actually done (not said) in the past to address those issues, and what their campaign strategy is to address these concerns now. Yet another story could be written about campaign finances—the cost of an average campaign, how the money will likely be spent, who finances campaigns, and what favors might be expected in return for contributions.

The reporter's objective is to 1) increase the viewer's/listener's understanding of how campaigns work, 2) to inform the public of the strategies used by each campaign so that the electorate can better distinguish reality from "hype," and 3) to find some new, interesting angles for election coverage.

Infotainment's Not All Bad

Challenge, competition, and fun are all words that competent professionals use to describe their careers. Humor has frequently been used to sharpen the focus on serious issues. For example, in the early 1980s people knowledgeable about nuclear weapons wanted to educate local public officials about the unworkability of the federally funded program that expected local government to provide safety through relocation for civilian populations in the event of nuclear war. They employed humor as their teacher. Community after community roared with laughter about the Federal Emergency Management Agency press release that suggested they could be safe if they dug a trench (through the asphalt) under their car, crawled in and sheltered themselves from the hurricane force winds with plastic tarps stretched from the car to the ground. Community after community learned about the characteristics of such a weapon, thought about the logistics of evacuation (in rush hour), and voted to oppose this program. No lecture series could have involved as many people or communicated a serious message so effectively.

Tell the Story behind the Candidate   This can be done with a "60 Minutes"-style personality focus. For example, in Moorhead, Minnesota, a single mother is spending time as campaign manager for first term State Rep. Diane Wray Williams. Who is she? Why is she doing this? This sounds like a personality to arouse audience curiosity. It suggests a tangible tie-in to how that office in the State Capitol affects the lives of constituents.

The Best Visuals Are Entertaining   Images are premium material for television. Some broadcasters consider their job simply as a conduit for the material given them by the candidate or official, making sure it gets on the air. Other reporters do the same thing by default. They don't have time to cover the story any other way. Some accept candidate-supplied material in order not to upset the incumbent and create an enemy for the station owners. Accepting candidate offered visuals is fine *if* the coverage does not disproportionately cover one candidate and *if* the visual images are not distortions of the record.

Enterprising broadcasters broaden their search for quality visuals. One suggestion for a station campaign plan is to tape each candidate at the onset of the campaign for use throughout the campaign in issue pieces; the same principle applies to gathering campaign images that are not time-bound and that can be used instead of "talking heads" throughout the campaign. For example, some of the candidates might have grassroot constituencies that hold newsworthy events, or come from neighborhoods where the camera can get interesting visuals that complement political topics covered by a reporter.

The initial interview of the candidate for issue footage might include some time spent on the candidate's professional and home turf shooting the candidate with family, neighbors, profession, and hobby. Find good visuals. Find entertaining visuals. But, when selecting which ones to air, remember Bill Moyers' query, "Isn't it the responsibility of the reporter to step back from the fray and compare image and record?"[34]

Referee the Game   As with sports events, the competition intensifies when the players are watched, reported upon, measured against standards, and whistled down if they break basic rules of fair play. That's entertaining and informative. It is also one key to quality campaign coverage. However, refereeing the campaign does not mean treating the campaign as a horse race, where who's ahead matters more than anything else. In a campaign, it is inappropriate to speculate about who's ahead until the voters have had their turn at the ballot box. In a campaign, sufficient investigative reporting allows you to have the information at hand to function as does a sportscaster. You broadcast the past records and the credentials of your athletes and their teams. Your time may be limited for such research, but planning ahead helps greatly. For example, the job could become relatively easy if one developed a station computer base with data comparing records and rhetoric on certain issues, listing past votes, a breakdown of district demographics, campaign contributor lists, and data from an annual report for the given government jurisdiction. Much of this material exists already (Sources are identified in Chapter 8). The data base might not be complete during the first election year, but as time passes it could become a valuable resource for the press. Stations and newspapers could develop a joint data bank and share such raw data. If this type of coverage is provided, in which the press can constantly verify candidate claims, campaigns will take on a different nature. Substance will matter. Truth and performance might matter too.

Sound-bites and Substance

Each passing year brings increasing criticism of nonsubstantive campaigners and superficial campaign coverage. In the 1988 presidential campaign neither the candidates nor the media addressed the 25 key issues facing the country. In fact less than 10% of the campaign coverage in 1988 covered issues of substance.[35]

Candidates need to alienate the fewest number of people. Therefore, they sometimes prefer generalities and trivia to substance that might be controversial. Broadcasters need to make sure that questions of interest to the public are answered by the

LINDA BOILEAU
Courtesy Frankfort State Journal

▶ *Figure 5   Soundbites and substance. Reprinted with permission of Linda Boileau, Frankfort,* State Journal, *Kentucky. ROTHCO.*

candidates. The problem for broadcasters is that American electronic media formats require short segments, and it takes considerable skill to fit substance into a short segment.

The skilled reporter will not only need to secure substantive answers from candidates aware that substance can be dangerous, but the reporter must find ways to pack this substance into a concise statement. The cooperative candidate will have learned, as exemplified by Jesse Jackson in the earlier illustration, that the sound-bite is often the most memorable way to convey a message in a short time. If the reporter is fortunate to have a candidate who has learned the art of sound-bite language, the reporter must still assess whether a given sound-bite is clever, funny, and, perhaps, substantive as well. Sometimes, clever and funny are worth covering, even if nonsubstantive.

A news story might be 20 seconds long. It might last 2 or 3 minutes. It's rare for it to be longer unless it's on CNN or a public broadcasting station. Critics frequently point out that this may be enough time for impressions; however, it is not enough time for issues. Obviously, a short segment cannot contain all the information one might convey on a given issue. But no single newspaper article, no single book, no 14-week college course, and no department of bureaucrats does justice to a given issue either. In addition, the personal attention span of the listener/viewer is limited for issues that may not be his immediate interest. Nonetheless, a reporter can provide substantive information using the vehicle of electronic media with its constraints on lengthy speech. The skill of the reporter depends on whether she thinks through the substance of the message to be broadcast. Otherwise the phrase "garbage in, garbage out" usually applied to computers, can be applied to the electronic media, as well.

A selected sound-bite can be stupid and meaningless or used to introduce a complex issue to a far larger audience than could be done through other forms of communication. "Where's the beef?," taken from a fast food commercial, was used by Walter Mondale against Gary Hart in the 1984 Democratic Presidential primaries. Whether it was valid or not, it did raise a general issue of criticism against Hart. Sound-bites can be used by the reporter to get audience attention for a more meaningful report. It would be followed by comments from a thoughtful person, a computer-graphic "primer" on the subject, appropriate visuals, and reporter comments. It is an important first step in the most widespread adult education known to self-government. In a 2-minute script the viewer can be provided an introduction to an issue and to the viewpoints of the candidates.

Stations interested in providing substantive coverage beyond what can be done in 2-minutes on-air news might consider the following. The listener/viewer can be given the opportunity to obtain more information. They could send stamped self-addressed envelopes and request a list of campaign offices where issue papers might be available, or a bibliography on the issue prepared by a local agency. The audience could hear a debate, participate in a talk show, read a newspaper calendar informing them about a lecture or a new book, or learn where to get government documents on performance to date on the issue. Adequate information should be accessible to those who want it. For many people, however, it is true that the brief electronic media introduction to the topic *is* sufficient.

Reporters also have some techniques available to them to counteract potential stonewalling on the part of candidates seeking to avoid substantive discussion. This evasiveness exists at the level of local and state campaigns, but it is most easily recognized through our common experience with national elections. In the 1984 election, national press corps reporters noted that they traveled 27,000 miles with President Reagan and never once got to ask him a question. When asked what to do about the stonewalling, one reporter commented, "You can't go on air and say he never holds news conference. The public wants news. I think what you have to put on air is information about Reagan's tax plan, his deficit reduction plan. Forget about the event of the day."[36] Another technique reporters can use to demand substance is for stations together to insist that they won't attend "photo ops" unless there are "question ops." If stations together can't succeed, then individual reporters need to be creative about covering other aspects of a campaign in their community and minimizing the air time devoted to the daily glitz.

Show Folks Inside the Gold Purse

If you want an x-ray of the candidate's strengths and weaknesses from the viewpoint of electability, not credentials, focus on the gold purse. Money provides the "threshold of recognition" that enables one to be a candidate. Money buys votes by providing name recognition, by bringing the candidate to the voters' homes through media advertising, mailings, pleasant events, and personal visits.

Increasingly, a candidate for any office that covers a jurisdiction of more than a few thousand population must spend the majority of her time raising money to fill the gold purse. Why not a media story in the time required for fundraising, time lost for issue work and constituent services?

Representative government is built on the idealistic notion of "representatives" of the population making the policy. Could you raise $25,000 every 2 years to serve your district of 18,000 voters as State Representative? Could you raise over a half million dollars every 2 years to be elected as your district's U.S. Representative in Congress? As the pressure builds, the poorer individuals drop out or find special interests to bankroll their campaign. Which special interests are bankrolling which candidates, and why? That's a story of far greater importance than the simple listing of donors. Candidates walk a real tightrope. They can lose the election without the contributions. They can lose their independence with the contributions. All too often, donors are expecting to buy something other than good government—a construction contract, a job, a vote to ease regulation of their business.

Don't forget the other gold purse—that of the taxpayer. What does the incumbent do with the public trust once elected? Andrea Mitchell not only found a way to inform the public on one aspect of the election finance process in the 1989 script, "Pork Barrel Politics," but to educate the public on the problems and on who makes decisions, turning what might have been another straight news story into a revealing mini-documentary enabling those who want to register their opinion on the process to know what the facts are and to know who makes the decisions. It certainly is not the role of broadcasters to suggest how the audience should respond, but it is most appropriate for broadcasters to make the mechanisms for participation available to one's viewers/listeners.

NAT SOT FULL...shots of Bevill on barge. . . disolve to college girl singing	"Tom Bevill, Tom Bevill, a legend in his time. Tom Bevill, Tom Bevill, a statesman in his prime."
VOICE-OVER	Tom who?
PUSH TO SIGN	He is not well known outside of Alabama. . . but they're singing his praises at Bevill Hall. . . at the Bevill Center for Advanced Manufacturing Technology. . . in Gadsden, Alabama.
Bevill Portrait on wall	
DISSOLVE to Bevill on Barge on Tenn-Tom Waterway	Tom Bevill is more than just another local on congressman. He is the King of Pork Barrel Projects. . . distributor of billions of dollars of what some call questionable water and energy projects to his home state. . . and the districts of his congressional allies.
SOT Rep. Tom Bevill D Alabama	"You know there's a good definition for pork and that's something that's in somebody else's congres sional district.
VOICE-OVER SHOTS of dams...	But at home, Tom Bevill is heralded for "bringing home the bacon". . .
Water projects	Diverting rivers.
	Digging out harbors.
	Building waterways...such as the Tenessee Tombigee.
	Known locally as "the Tenn-Tom"...it is classic pork:
	A two-billion dollar inland water system hated by environmentalists...but supported by local businessmen. It was created with Bevill's help to compete with the Mississippi River for cargo traffic.
	How does Bevill do it?
	Through years of seniority. . . He's become a leading member of the House Appropriations Committee: the powerful overlords of Federal spending known on Capital Hill as the College of Cardinals.
Appropriations meeting	Meeting behind closed doors, rarely photographed. . . They divide up shrinking resources. Making sure to take care of their districts.
SOT Tom Bevill	"Somebody has to make the decisions, so we on the Appropriations make the decisions."

▶ *Figure 6*   *Pork Barrel Politics. Reprinted courtesy of Andrea Mitchell, Chief Congressional Correspondent, NBC News, Washington, D.C.*

VOICE-OVER committee	They sure do.
DISSOLVE to map with thirty	For instance. . .
DOTS for pork projects	This year. . .after agreeing to begin no new water or energy projects. . . committee mem bers added thirty of them.
	Billions of dollars deemed unnecessary by the Army Corps of Engineers.
	The Bush Administration wanted none of these projects. . . but didn't complain.
(CHANGE PICTURE) AERIALS of supercollider location	That's because the committee made sure to put in money for the President's pet pork project. . . the multi-billion dollar super-collider for Texas.
STANDUP Bridge	That's the kind of tradeoff that makes Bevill so powerful here in the halls of Congress.
	But these days...the system of trading on pork projects is coming under increasing attack:
SOT Michael Waldman Congress Watch

Cover with pix of Tenn-Tom Waterway | "Where money goes shouldn't necessarily be determined by where powerful members of Congress happen to live but by what serves the best interests of the country. Pork Barrel is as old as the Congress itself, the problem is that now with federal dollars drying up it becomes more and more important in determining how federal money is spent." |
SOT Rep. Leon Panetta Budget Chairman	"As that pie shrinks, there is a tremendous battle going on here over priorities and over Members' interests in their districts."
VOICE-OVER Gadsen, Alabama scene	Don't tell that to satisfied folks back home. . . where Democrats and Republicans alike view Tom Bevill as a hero:
SOT Lewis Fuller Republican City Council Member	"That's a job that a Congressman has is to try to return as many tax dollars as possible to his district and in that regard Mr. Bevill has done an excellent job"
VOICE-OVER set up interview	It's the kind of power built on years of seniority:
SOT Rep. Tom Bevill	"When I came to Congress, I didn't like the se- niority system, I didn't think much of it, but the longer I stay here, I think it's good, I support it (Big Grin)
SOT of Bevill song over more pix of waterway	"With his expertise and his pleasant smile, he makes the Tenn-Tom flow. He's a country gent who can't be bent, Tom Bevill's on the go.
	Andrea Mitchell, NBC News, Washington

▶ *Figure 6*   *(continued)*

Quality reporting on this aspect of campaigns could ease the pressure on candidates, save the taxpayer from costly and unwise policy decisions, and lead to serious public discussion of reforming campaign finance systems that result in special interests excluding the citizenry from the political process.

AWARDS

As a new century approaches, major advances will occur in election coverage techniques. Creative and able reporters will be responsible for most of these innovations. The challenge for the broadcaster is summarized by Bill Moyers: "Some journalists can inform and nurture the public mind. They figure out how to point out the nuances, to hold conventional wisdom to public scrutiny. Without that [type of journalism], we're at the mercy of the politicians whose goal is to win, and we're at the mercy of the corporations whose goal is to get rich."[37]

Many institutions sponsor rewards for outstanding broadcasting. Hopefully, some of you will win awards for your excellence in election coverage. Below is a partial list.[38]

1. Scripps Howard Foundation National Journalism Awards, for excellence in a program or a series of programs designed to promote the public good, Cincinnati, OH.
2. Allen H. Neuharth Award for Excellence in Journalism, University of South Dakota, Vermillion, SD.
3. Edward R. Murrow Awards for Excellence in Electronic Journalism,Columbia University, NY.
4. The George Foster Peabody Awards for "Broadcasting's Best," University of Georgia College of Journalism and Mass Communication.
5. Freedom Foundation's award to educate Americans about their responsibility as citizens in a free society, Rt. 23, Valley Forge, PA., 19481.
6. Community Action Network Award to honor media for the best coverage of solutions to community problems, 211 E. 43rd St., Suite 1400, NY, NY, 10017.
7. International Radio and Television Society, Broadcaster of the Year Award, NY.
8. EMMA (Exceptional Merit in Media) Awards from the National Women's Political Caucus, Washington D.C.
9. Gold Medal Winners for best public service announcement given out by the International Advertising Association and the New York Festivals, NY, NY.
10. Radio, Television News Directors Association regional awards for spot news, for news series and documentaries, for investigative reporting, for continuing coverage,Washington, D.C.
11. National Commendation Awards for those who work to improve the image of women in radio and television, sponsored by American Women in Radio and Television, Washington, D.C.
12. "Outstanding Local Television Broadcasting" IRIS awards presented by National Association of Television Program Executives, Los Angeles, CA.

13. National Association of Broadcasters Awards for significant and lasting achievement in American broadcasting, Washington, D.C.
14. Mobius Awards from the United States TV and Radio Commercials Festival for excellence in advertising. Elmhurst, IL.
15. Innovator of the Year Award by National Broadcast Association for Community Affairs.
16. National Broadcast Editorial Association award for excellence in writing and presenting editorials, Los Angeles, CA.
17. Trustees Award for outstanding contribution to the advancement of television by a person, organization, or group of people from the National Academy of Television Arts and Sciences, Burbank, CA.
18. Alfred I. DuPont Columbia University Award for excellence in broadcast journalism.
19. Fourth Estate Award from the American Legion for outstanding achievement in journalism. Indianapolis, IN.
20. "NAPB Awards" from Associated Press Broadcasters for outstanding AP reports, Washington, D.C.
21. Edward R. Murrow Brotherhood Awards from B'nai B'rith for the best news production promoting human understanding, NY.
22. University of Missouri awards for investigative reporting.
23. Unity Awards in Media from Lincoln University for outstanding coverage of minority affairs, St. Louis, MO.
24. Livingston Awards from the Mollie Parmis Livingston Foundation for a single news report or a series done by a young journalist, Ann Arbor, MI.
25. Washington Correspondents Award from the National Press Club for reporting Washington news for hometown listeners, Washington, D.C.
26. Newsletter Journalism Award from the National Press Club for analytical interpretive reporting and exclusive reporting,Washington, D.C.
27. Louis M. Lyons Award from the Nieman Foundation at Harvard University for conscience and integrity in journalism.
28. Robert F. Kennedy Journalism Awards from the RFK Memorial Committee for outstanding coverage of the problems of the disadvantaged, Washington D.C..
29. Society for Professional Journalism "Distinguished Service Award" for the best journalistic effort of the year. Chicago, IL.
30. Clarion Awards from Women in Communications, Inc., for excellence in all areas of broadcasting, Arlington, VA.
31. Armstrong Awards for excellence and originality in news, news documentaries, community service, creative use of the medium, from the Armstrong Foundation in cooperation with Columbia University, NY.
32. Avatar Award from the Broadcast Financial Management Association for outstanding contributions to the financial side of the communications industry. Des Plains, IL.
33. Gold Medallion Awards from the Broadcast Promotion and Marketing Executives, Inc., for special promotion projects, San Diego State University, San Diego, CA.

34. Jack R. Howard Broadcast Awards from Scripps-Howard Foundation for single program or series to promote the public good. Mushsgee, OH.
35. Annual Awards for Investigative Reporting sponsored by Investigative Reporters and Editors, Jan Colbert, Columbia, MO.
36. Lowell Mellett Award for Improving Journalism through Critical Evaluation, through the School of Communications at Pennsylvania State University, University Park, PA.
37. Madison Award for those who work to preserve freedom of expression based on National Broadcast Editorial Association selection, WKYC-TV, Cleveland, OH, .and Awards for Editorial Excellence, c/o KBIG–FM, Los Angeles, CA.
38. The Ohio State Awards for excellence in education, informational and public affairs broadcasting, Columbus, OH.
39. Penny-Missouri Awards for community leadership for those stations who address community problems through the University of Missouri–Columbia, St. Louis, MO.

Notes

1. "Campaigning on Cue," produced after the 1984 election by WTTW-TV, Chicago for the William Benton Fellowship's University of Chicago Conference.
2. "News Anchors Address the Power of the Chair," *Broadcasting*, March 23, 1987, p.136.
3. Personal interview with Andrea Mitchell, NBC Chief Congressional Correspondent, Washington, D.C., February 14, 1990.
4. Ibid.
5. Chuck Crouse, "Just Who Is a Reporter, Anyway?" *RTNDA Communicator*, November 1985, p. 14.
6. Ibid.
7. Earl R. Hutchinson, Sr., *Writing for Mass Communication* (New York: Longman, 1986).
8. David G. Clark, "News for Television," Ibid, 269.
9. Ibid., 270.
10. Interview with Mitchell.
11. Walter Karp, "All the Congressmen's Men," *Harpers,* July 1989.
12. Ibid., 58.
13. Extra, *The Newsletter of Fairness and Accuracy in Reporting*, 2, no. 2 (September/October 1988): p. 4.
14. Chuch Crouse, "Reporting for Radio," *RTNDA Communicator*, December 1986, p. 28.
15. Sen. Edward Kennedy, "Beyond `Entertainment Tonight': The Press and the 1988 Campaign," *Institute of Politics Newsletter* 1, no. 2 (Winter 1988).
16. Charles Krauthammer, "Media Scorecard," *Washington Post*, February 19, 1988.
17. Michael Oreskes, "America's Politics Loses Way as Its Vision Changes World," *New York Times*, March 18, 1990, p. 1.
18. Ross Gelbspan, "Study: Media in Boston Reinforce Racism by News Coverage Decisions," *Boston Globe*, January 28, 1987. The study was done by Kirk Johnson, associate editor of *East-West Journal.*
19. *Black Elected Officials: A National Roster*, Joint Center for Political Studies Press,

Washington, D.C., 1988, p. 13–14.

20. *1989 National Roster of Hispanic Elected Officials*, National Association of Latino Elected and Appointed Officials, Washington, D.C., 1989, p. vi.

21. Ruth Mandel, Director of Center for the American Woman and Politics, Eagleton Institute of Politics, Rutgers University, speech delivered at Kennedy Library Conference, Boston, May 1, 1987.

22. Sandra Baxter and Marjorie Lansing, *Women and Politics: The Invisible Majority* (Ann Arbor: University of Michigan Press, 1980), 142.

23. Bella Abzug, *Gender Gap* (Boston: Houghton Mifflin, 1984), 172.

24. Ruth Mandel, *In the Running: The New Woman Candidate* (New York: Ticknor and Fields, 1981), 53.

25. Jeane Kirkpatrick, *Political Woman* (New York: Basic Books, 1974), 223.

26. Personal correspondence and interview with former U.S. Senator Mike Gravel.

27. Austin Ranney *Channels of Power: The Impact of Television on American Politics* (New York: Basic Books, 1983), 171–172.

28. Chuck Crouse, "Reporter's Journal" WEEI News Radio, Boston , July 26–27, 1987.

29. Marty Linsky, *Television and the Presidential Elections* (Lexington MA.: Lexington Books, Quote from Congressperson David Obey (D-WI), 1983), 22.

30. Ruth B. Mandel, *In the Running*, 57.

31. Oreskes, "America's Politics Loses, 22.

32. Interview with Mitchell.

33. Personal interview with Chuck Crouse, Boston reporter, WEEI, News(CBS affliated all-news radio), January 30, 1990.

34. Bill Moyers, "Image and Reality in America, *The Public Mind*, WGBH, Boston, November 22, 1989.

35. Ibid.

36. Interview with Mitchell.

37. Bill Moyers, "Image and Reality in America," *The Public Mind*, WGBH, Boston, December 5, 1989.

38. See *Broadcasting and Cable Yearbook* (Washington, D.C.: Broadcasting Publications, 1989), p. F–38–41. Also see RTNDA, *Intercom*, January 5, 1989.

4

▼ Political Advertising

IMAGE INFORMATION

The average person is exposed to 2,700 commercial images daily. Within this barrage of images and information candidates are trying to introduce new products—themselves. Being noticed in this clutter of images requires remarkable saturation. The competition is not so much the other candidates, but all the images collectively.[1]

The craft of marketing candidates through television commercials is over 25 years old. But its popularity among winning candidates seems unstoppable. It molds the images that win. For example, a 30-second spot produced by media consultant Dan Payne[2] for Congressperson Les Au Coin of Oregon concentrated on the image of a Representative who is directly responsible for the economic growth of his constituency. The ad showed and attributed four areas of economic progress to Congressperson Au Coin: helicopters, highway dollars, mill jobs, and shipbuilding contracts. The tag for the commercial says "Results for Oregon—Les Au Coin." While the commercial presents substance rather than appearance, it is the acceptance of the substance as true that reinforces the appearance or image. The same claims could be made in a spot without citing and attributing specific areas of economic growth to the candidate, but merely presenting the concept in generalities. This ad strengthens both aspects.

Another 30-second spot by Payne concentrates totally on appearance, without any implication of facts, yet can be just as effective in creating an image. It opens with shots of crowded New York subways and streets and counterpoints with a peaceful Vermont scene; it follows with a traffic jam in Massachusetts and then shows another peaceful Vermont scene; it then contrasts crowded streets and beaches in New Hampshire with an idyllic shot of a Vermont lake. "This is Vermont," a voice-over narrator says. "And this is how we keep it that way. Madelaine Kunin. Good for Vermont." (She was elected governor.) Without any substance, we have an effective image of the Governor as the person who preserves the quality of life for her state, Vermont.

Image, more than information, is the essence of modern American culture. When you think of former President Richard Nixon or former President Jimmy Carter or of Albert Einstein, a face comes to mind—not words. Educator Neil Postman's point is valid: we're an "image-centered culture," not "word-centered."[3]

Images are powerful tools of persuasion. They may or may not be true. Their purpose is to convince, not to inform. These ads are critical to any modern-day

American campaign in a district of more than 2,500 voters. An analysis of campaign-spot advertisement strategy tells the reporter:

1. The highest priority for allocation of candidate funds;
2. The message that the candidate wants the voters to hear;
3. Which voters the message is (or is not) for;
4. What investigative research does (or does not) prove about opposing candidates;
5. How much candidates are spending to "buy" name recognition, which translates into votes;
6. How the money race goes between eligible candidates;
7. Who the money comes from, and what the donor hopes to "buy" with a contribution.

The news branch of broadcasting has, in the past, paid minimal attention to political advertising. To continue to do so is no longer appropriate. The technological tools are changing so quickly that the style of advertising in the 1990s, and its impact, has little resemblance to advertising in 1960s and is even different than that of only a few years ago. According to Merv Weston, a longtime political advertising consultant and founder of Weston Advertising, "until 1960, the New Hampshire Primary candidate used full page newspaper advertisements and radio ads. The 1968 Eugene McCarthy campaign strategy was to saturate every little radio station in New Hampshire with 60 second spots, twelve to fifteen times a day, with the Senator's voice talking about ending the Viet Nam War, and about other social democrat issues such as the elderly and the poor. The ads cost $6 each. Things weren't much different until the late seventies—in part because New Hampshire didn't have viable *local* television stations. By the 1980's television took over, and so did the 'Washington Boys' (the campaign handlers)."

Now, all the candidates, even for the Senate and Congress, use a small bank of Washington, D.C. accepted "experts" for opposition research, polling, direct mail, and for their media advertising. It's not always wise for the candidate. Sometimes local people understand the local market and can work with local stations far better than persons working by phone hundreds of miles away."[4]

ADVERTISING AND MONEY

The campaign advertising coin has two sides. One is the revenue to the station. The other is the cost to a democratic society requiring self-government. The National Association of Broadcasters' data indicates that station revenue in 1988, a presidential campaign year, was a relatively small percent of station revenue.

FM radio	under 1% of net revenue
AM radio	under 2% of net revenue
TV affiliates	3.6% of net revenue
TV independents	1.6% of net revenue[5]

To put the spending in perspective, *USA Today* notes that in the 1984 presidential campaign the $325 million spent by candidates on television advertising was but a fraction of the $2.4 billion that the nation's three top commercial advertisers, Proctor and Gamble, General Motors, and Sears spent on 1984 television ads[6]—but, then candidates aren't corporations.

Local TV Stations
For the 1980s decade, candidates have spent considerably more money on local station ads than on network ads. For example:

Year	Network	Local
1980	$ 20,699,700	$ 69,114,300
1982	861,900	122,760,300
1984	43,652,500	110,171,500
1986	459,300	161,184,000 [7]

Local Radio Stations
While often eclipsed by television, advertising on radio is of some interest to candidate media advisors. An NAB report of the first study undertaken of radio political advertising effectiveness indicates that in 11 winning mayoral races in New Mexico in 1986, radio political advertising was an important ingredient. The NAB report reminds us that the average household has 5.4 radios, that 56% of adults hear the news first each morning via their radio, that 95% of all cars have radios, and that 75% of adults can be reached by car radio during an average week.[8]

In smaller towns and rural areas radio reaches audiences most effectively, depending on the time segment. For example, WGIR Radio in New Hampshire has 10,000 listeners at 8 A.M. weekdays, and only 2,000 at 9 A.M. In large districts, radio buys may be somewhat controversial for two reasons: 1) as radio stations move into narrowcasting (that is, farm shows, or ethnic shows), the audience may be so narrow that even though advertising costs are cheap one may not get the best "bang for the buck"; 2) drive time, while reaching a large audience, may be too broad in target and too ambiguous about who is reached for the dollars spent.[9] Some media consultants believe that because radio has more predictable and loyal audiences (demographically pinpointed) radio ads are useful supplements to television in order to be sure that the right demographic audience is reached. So a "vertical message" to a specialized audience is purchased.[10]

Cable Television Stations
In 1990, cable reached the 60% penetration mark, installed in about 54 million American homes. Cable and the three TV networks each account for about one-third of the viewers watching television. In addition, cable subscribers are 24% more likely to vote than non-cable subscribers.[11] In the second half of the 1980s overall cable advertising revenue jumped from $58 million to $767 million, based on figures distributed by the Television Bureau of Advertising[12]. The 1990 decade will likely see comparable increases in cable political advertising revenue.

Cable television advertising becomes more and more important. Cable's flexibility and local appeal are attractive to candidates for local offices, and to those seeking office in larger jurisdictions who want to target a particular message to a particular demographic group. Furthermore, spots on cable are not limited to 15 or

30 seconds, but may be several minutes in length. In 1988 the Nielsen Media Research corporation and the National Cable Television Association merged their data base to produce on-line service capable of identifying cable advertising possibilities by Congressional district, complete with a demographic index and a listing of open ad slots.[13] Using computer technology to produce improved market date will alter the media consultant's view of cable. Until now, many political advertisers were not sure what they were getting in cable.

One example of effective candidate use of cable is Bill Bradley's 1988 race for reelection to the Senate from New Jersey. New Jersey relies on stations in New York and Philadelphia for its broadcast television. Consequently, New Jersey news isn't top priority, and station rates are based on reaching audience far larger than Bradley needed. Bradley's experience indicated that his local cable ads increased his poll ratings. His best cable spots were on CNN and ESPN, whose audiences, it was determined, are likely to vote.[14]

Station Revenue Summary

Political advertising revenue does matter to the local station. Every election cycle there is guaranteed revenue to stations without any marketing cost. All the work is done by media-buying firms, and all the station sales staff does is collect checks. It is all handled professionally and well in advance of broadcast time.[15]

One area of controversy among the broadcasting industry, the FCC, and Congress is the "lowest unit cost" regulation, whereby candidates are billed at the lowest rate for ads placed during the campaign (see details in Chapter 9). This regulation does affect the amount of revenue a station receives from political advertising. As pressure builds for changes in campaign finance laws, the industry, Congress, and public interest lobbyists will be required to find appropriate answers to the questions of why, whether, and to what extent the broadcast industry has responsibility to subsidize campaigns if other industries (such as printing, and airlines) are not required to do so.

Station management must look at election coverage within the context of overall business management. Determine whether the best payoff for the station is to consider the contribution to election coverage to be limited to providing advertising slots at reduced rates, or is it worthwhile strengthening the station's overall campaign coverage within the context of local news in order to strengthen the station's local news constituency, improve its news ratings, and enhance its local news commercial revenue. This determination can be made by evaluating the effect each aspect of coverage has on increasing station audience, and evaluating whether expanded news coverage can produce more advertising revenue for the station than can campaign advertising revenue.

POLITICAL AD COSTS TO CANDIDATES

Federal Elections

In the past 20 years media advertising has become arguably one of the most important methods for candidates to reach voters with their message. Why else would candidates allocate such a large portion of their campaign expenditures to it? Simultaneously, the cost of democracy has increased dramatically. Fixed-rate prime-time television advertising slots cost twice as much in 1988 as they did in 1982, yet during the same period the Consumer Price Index rose only about 25%.[16] The broadcast industry feels that efforts to blame it for ever increasing campaign costs is "to blame the messenger for the number of messages."[17]

Total advertising costs for 1986 House and Senate seats were tabulated by the National Association of Broadcasters:[18]

House
Billboards	$1.6m	.8% of whole
Radio	$10.2m	4.8% of whole
Print	$12.3m	5.8% of whole
TV	$23.1m	10.9% of whole

Senate
Billboards	$227t	.12% of whole
Radio	$1.1m	.60% of whole
Print	968t	.51% of whole
TV	$62.7m	33.09% of whole

If these costs are recalculated to include the production cost but not the media-consultant cost, the NAB totals show that candidates for the House spend an average of 19.8% of their campaign budget on radio and television advertising, while candidates for the Senate spent an average of 39.2%. An NAB survey showed that in the 1988 Congressional elections Senate candidates spent an average of 43.5% of their budgets for specific radio and TV time and that House candidates spent 19.8% of their budgets for the same—not including production costs, time-buyers fees, or related costs.[19]

Critics of the NAB study say that the cost for television and radio advertising is in fact much higher because these figures average the amount spent over all races and do not account for the fact that expense need not be great in uncontested races. Some estimate that well over 50% of a Congressional campaign budget is spent on broadcast media advertising.

In the presidential race the dollars spent on television ads are an even larger piece of the total campaign cost. In the primaries, in 1984, according to *USA Today* only 15% of the campaign budget was used for TV ads, but, in the general election, 55% of the total cost was for television ads.

State and Local Elections

Candidates for mayor and governor advertise in ways similar to that of congressional candidates. Candidates for county offices, state legislatures, and sometimes local council, and local offices, have historically used print media, but broadcast expenditures are growing, especially in cable.

For example, Diane Wray Williams was elected State Representative from Moorhead, Minnesota in 1988. She won her challenge campaign with 6,749 of the 13,303 votes cast. Even in a small district, she bought broadcast television time. Of the $23,000 she spent to get elected, 50% was spent on media advertising. "It struck me as bizarre to pay so much for so little," Williams stated, "but, when I knocked on voters' doors, it seemed to make a difference when they said 'I just saw you on television.'"[20]

Candidates Are Not Corporations.

Pricey campaigns affect the quality of government for all of us—broadcaster and citizen alike. Several decades ago, when Robert Kennedy was Attorney General, he made the following observation about a situation that has only grown worse since: "The mounting costs of elections is rapidly becoming intolerable for a democratic society, where the right to vote and to be a candidate is the ultimate political protection. We are in danger of creating a situation in which our candidates must be chosen only from among the rich, the famous, or those willing to be beholden to others to pay the bills." [21]

Congressional incumbents spent an average of $370,000 per race while challengers spent $135,000. For a challenger to be on a par as an equal competitor, name recognition is required. Media consultant studies show that a typical congressional candidate must buy 750 gross rating points in each media market to achieve the minimum name recognition needed to match an incumbent. This alone could cost from $84,000 to $361,000 depending on the media market.[22]

For the broadcast industry, the purchase of campaign ads not only increases station revenue but fosters an environment where public policy, including such areas as health, environment, and education, might be viewed as a commodity purchased for the highest campaign contribution, rather than as laws emerging from careful and reasoned analysis of the situation. This situation is manifest through candidate reliance on PAC contributions as the source of necessary campaign funds. PACs are the only legal way for special interest groups to organize for concentrated electoral activity. Some of these PACs represent public interest concerns, like the environment or education, but most PACs are industry-based, expecting actions from government officials that will favor their industry in return for the campaign contributions. PAC contributions are also the only way to secure sums greater than that possible from individual donors. How else can candidates raise the funds needed? The Washington- based public interest group Common Cause notes, "The average successful candidate for U.S. Senate spent some $4m—which means that said Senator is obliged to raise $12,000 per week for each week of his/her 6 year term. Incumbents have an easier time securing PAC funds needed to raise large enough campaign coffers, consequently, in 1988, 98% of the incumbent Senators and House members who sought reelection were reelected."[23]

These sums are enormous for the individual candidates even at the "lowest unit rate." But according to a 1990 FCC audit of radio and television stations, most of the stations did not understand the "lowest unit cost" requirement and were over charging.[24] The high cost of media advertising can not be interpreted the same way for individuals seeking office as they are for corporations selling products. The "investment" return is not comparable. The corporation intends to recoup its advertising costs in sales to the public. The only thing a candidate has to sell to recover the cost of advertising is her subsequent "vote" on public policy decisions. Democracy cannot thrive if personal gain must substitute for public well-being.

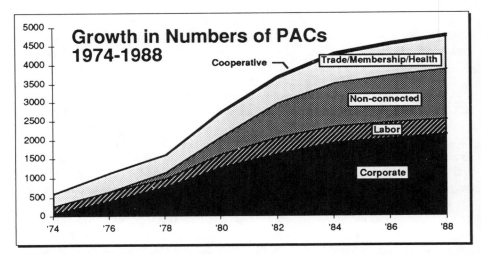

▶ *Figure 7   The impact of PACs. Source: Larry Makinson*, The Price of Admission
(Washington D.C.: Center for Responsive Politics, 1989), p. 14, drawing on Vital Statistics
of Congress 1987–1988 (Congressional Quarterly) *and Federal Election Commission.*

A new phenomenon to watch is the mailing of candidate video tapes to carefully selected voters. For the first time, in the early 1990s some candidates are choosing the VCR over the station ad. They say they can reach as many.voters for less
cost. To mail one tape cost less than $5.

The chart illustrates the rapidly increasing number of PACs and the increasing
percentage of campaign revenues that comes from PACs.

THE ADS THEMSELVES

Short Attention Span: Short Message

Political media consultant Dan Payne warns that "people will no more tune in a
half hour of politics than they will a half hour Chevy commercial. The droning on is
listened to only by partisans and reporters. In a half-hour show, candidates will be
carefully scripted and cautious. And, when the half hour is over, the reporters only
report on a single sound bite of it anyway."[25]

This concern is reinforced by educator Neil Postman: "People of a television
culture need "plain language" both aurally and visually,—The Gettysburg Address
would have been largely incomprehensible to a [modern] audience."[26]

And Professor Robert Manoff says, "It's not information which is a scarce
commodity anymore. It's attention—because humans have a limit. To get attention
for social decision making, there have to be restraints on information."[27]

The trick, then, is to design an ad that gets one's attention and creates an image
and/or communicates an important substantive message in 30 seconds. One such ad
created by Dan Payne opposes military waste and urges support for a candidate at the
same time. The spot opens on U.S. Senator John Kerry in an ordinary hardware
store. He compares the regular costs of pieces of hardware with the price the Pentagon paid for the same item: a 22-cent plaster cap for which the Pentagon paid
$1,100, a 20-cent collar wrench that cost the Pentagon $9,000, and a 10-cent diode

that the Pentagon bought for $110 . Kerry says, "Anybody who thinks you have to spend like this to keep America strong must have a screw loose." The graphic tag states: "John Kerry—A Senator You Can Trust." This spot uses substance—specific information—as the base for creating a strong, concerned, trustworthy image.

Another Payne ad with a short message is designed to present the Mayor of a city as responsible for getting jobs for his constituents. What can you do in 30 seconds? Coleman Young, Mayor of Detroit, is shown at a building construction site. While building activity is going on behind him, Young stresses how his efforts have kept construction going in Detroit, resulting in more and more jobs. The spot ends with the graphics: "Mayor Young. Detroit's future is in good hands." Presuming that the viewers are convinced that the Mayor is indeed responsible for continuing building construction in Detroit, they then accept the image of someone who continues to get them jobs.

Some media consultants will tell you that the art of 30-second political spots is in its infancy. As one consultant, Ken Swope, says, "It's possible to create powerful images. The issue now is how to juxtapose those images with words so that the words matter as much as possible. If image is very strong, people say they don't hear words. But, maybe they do. Maybe such a spot has a longer lasting value in that with repetition, a person sees and hears more each time. A dramatic image and text can convey substance.[28] Another consultant, Dan Payne, puts it this way, "Long commercials create voter/viewer fatigue. Ads intrude. Viewers want to watch programs."[29] And veteran media consultant Merv Weston states, "People won't listen to substance. They don't understand it. They don't vote for it. They vote for personalities. People voted for Reagan for psychological reasons—a grandfather image. The country is not more conservative, or more liberal. It's more superficial. A thoughtful candidate can't win unless he can convey their message in a sound-bite. No one has the time or patience for the long speech or the issue paper."[30]

Brevity is not necessarily inadequacy. As illustrated above, significant images and information can be communicated concisely. Similarly, it is inappropriate to assume that length itself guarantees significant information. Long spots, interviews, or debates can sometimes generate more heat than light.

The point is that political advertising has become a fact of life in America. The most vociferous academic objections to this form of communication will not cause it to disappear. A whole generation of Americans consider political ads to be the primary means of campaigning. They have come to expect information in "sound-bites" It may not be the best way to provide election coverage, but it may not be the worst. We are being smothered in excess information on everything imaginable; most of it has become relatively meaningless. In this environment, these powerful campaign advertising images get the public's attention. That can be a worthwhile step toward positive communication.

Our objective is to provide full and fair election coverage to the voters/audience that presently exists—not to change the attention span or mode of learning of the public to something that it was in Lincoln's time, or might be in another society. Rather than lamenting the constraints of the medium, learn to harness this remarkable technology so that its images can have substance, and so that its messages can evoke a response. It is frequently stated that nothing of substance can be addressed in

30 seconds. We forget that the entire Gettysburg Address took but 2 minutes. A broadcast news story will run from 20 seconds to 3 minutes.

Lack of substance in political advertising cannot be blamed totally on the length of the ad. To be substantive in 30 seconds is clearly very difficult, but not impossible. Ads that are 1, 2, and 3 minutes long offer greater opportunity for the creative media consultant, provided the candidate can afford it and the station accepts nonconventional-length ads. The lack of substance often lies with the producer of the ad. Sometimes candidates want an ad to respond to what the polls tell them makes the voter "feel good" rather than to convey their programmatic message. Sometimes candidates intentionally use an ad to criticize their opponent rather than to communicate their message.

Michael Dukakis, himself the target of highly successful negative ads in the 1988 presidential election campaign, effectively used a very creative Dan Payne ad against a primary opponent. The spot shows a character, designated as Representative Richard Gephart, doing somersaults in alternating directions. The voice-over narrator states that Gephart has done flip-flops on a number of issues, such as being for and against Reaganomics, and for and against raising the minimum wage. It shows the Gephart TV character in a boxing pose, with the narrator stating that Gephart acts tough toward corporations, but takes their PAC money. The ad then states that Michael Dukakis refuses PAC money. "You know where Mike Dukakis stands, but Congressman Gephardt, he's still up in the air," as the visual freezes on a still frame of the Gephardt character suspended in air in the middle of a somersault. Whether the substantive comments are true or not is irrelevant; the satirical portrayal of Gephardt creates a negative image of him in the eyes of the viewers.

Negative Advertising

"Commercial speech" is protected by the U. S. Constitution only if it is truthful. However, "political speech" is protected in all circumstances, provided there is no malice.[31] In ads where the candidate makes the attack or makes an appearance, Section 315 of the Federal Communications Act prohibits any broadcaster censorship of the advertisement (see Chapter 9). If the candidate does not appear, there is no obligation for the station to air the ad. In fact, political ads are not protected from libel suits. If a product ad is false, misleading, or deceptive, the station may have to answer to the Federal Trade Commission or the Federal Communication Commission.

While there is no "truth in political advertising" law, why not ask ourselves whether a political ad would appear on our stations if subjected to the same standards applied to product ads. If a candidate wants certain extreme material on the air, perhaps it is best that he be directly associated with the material, at least to the degree that he appears on the ad in a way which makes it a "use" under Section 315."[32] One problem is that sometimes truth is a value judgment rather than a fact. Sometimes, especially in negative campaigning, lies are not explicit but they are lies through innuendo.

The NAB suggested to Congress that one way to help curb negative campaign tactics would be to require candidates to appear in at least 50% of each of their own commercials in order to qualify for "lowest unit rate." Now only a one-line tag or a tiny photo at the end of a commercial is required.[33] The NAB agrees that negative ads turn off the American public, but the FCC mandates that the industry cannot censor material in a broadcast ad that includes an appearance by a candidate unless it is clearly obscene or indecent. However the station may review and edit material to be broadcast by a candidate's supporter.

AD PLACEMENT

Getting the Best Audience

One political advertising agency indicated that 70 to 80% of media dollars spent by the firm is targeted for "news adjacencies." Most stations won't run political spots within the news because it could be perceived as news bias. For example, if a news story is on pollution and is followed by an ad on the environment, one could argue that viewers might make biased interpretations. Also, spots within the news broadcast are not difficult to sell to commercial advertisers at full price. While a sitcom may have more viewers than does the news, news watchers are more likely voters. After news adjacencies, ad firms seek placements designed to reach their targeted constituency. For example, if they want to reach segments of the female population, they might place ads with the Phil Donahue show, or, if their demographics indicate they need to reach men over 50, they buy football.[34]

Most political advertisements are in September and October, just when new shows begin, when Christmas shopping ads increase, and when general rates go up. Even though political ads are at the lowest rate, it is still higher in the fall than it would have been in January. In addition, a station will limit the number of news adjacencies bought for a given candidate. During the last 3 to 6 weeks before election day, a candidate may be allowed to purchase only 2, 3, or 4 per week, total. Whereas had a candidate known about this pending restriction earlier and avoided it by purchasing ads earlier, she might have bought a greater number. Some stations place the same kind of limits on prime-time ads. The station decision is made by the Station Manager and the Business Manager. Sometimes political considerations affect the decision. For example, if station management favors the incumbent, they might place limits on the ads placed for the challenger.[35]

The issue for the candidates and their handlers is to be sure that they can have qualitative value in rating points comparable to that offered other candidates. "Don't tell me I'll get the same benefit from 'Hogan's Heroes' that someone else can get from 'Cosby'."[36]

Broadcaster's Role

Stations are beginning to see political advertising as a force in the market. Some ad firms report calls from station salespeople many months before an election. What's happening this year? How much money do you think Kerry will spend on his Senate race this year? The ad agencies see this early planning as good. Political advertising revenue is easy money for the station even though broadcasters dislike the rate protection. Candidates can make life miserable for a station if, without planning, there's a request for a lot of ads at the last minute. Similarly, federal candidates, with the FCC protections, can cause time-consuming problems for a station if their needs are not met. Stations want to be responsive to mayoral candidates. Mayors have some immediate hold over station in terms of access to news information. Dan Payne, Boston-based media consultant, says, "We're all getting used to the volume of media advertising; stations no longer view politicians as once a year step children. Everyone sits down together to figure out how to make the placements work."[37]

Stations, by law, must sell to all candidates equally. But sometimes station irregularity can be criticized as favoritism. One could show favoritism by allowing someone in at the last minute and letting them put a spot into rotation on the Friday night before Tuesday's election and then either refuse the other candidate at such a late date or not let the other candidate know. The station can be vulnerable to such charges. But the election will be over before they are made. It is in the self-interest of stations wishing to avoid bureaucratic hassles to make a rule about deadlines, stick to it, and be sure opponents are given time to respond.[37]

Similarly, station sales personnel need to be cautious about the ethics of selling space. Going to one candidate to encourage purchases based on a rival's purchases is questionable and may be interpreted as trafficking. The time salesperson may even reveal what kind of buy is being made by the opposition (such as news or the "Cosby Show"). Stations should have clear policies of how such information may be made public, whether through the station log or from a sales agent. What's fair for one must be fair for all.[38]

SELLING SOAP: SELLING SURVIVAL

In the United States, political advertising is here to stay. Speculation about abolishing it may make an interesting discussion but it won't make a difference in our election coverage in the foreseeable future. Just as we're learning to use the products of other new technologies, it is time to recognize that political advertising can't be ignored. The Constitution has no problem ignoring soap-selling. Let the market decide.

On the other hand, when it comes to preserving fair and full discussion of the ingredients of self-government, the situation differs. Consider folding coverage of advertisements into coverage of the news. Consider establishing common guidelines for all advertisers. Consider promoting truth in advertising, not alone on ethical grounds but because your station will have better quality, more stimulating coverage, better ratings, and more commercial advertising. The bottom line of the station well-being as well as that of its audience will be strengthened as the process of electoral self-government is strengthened.

Notes

1. Personal interview with Merv Weston, founder and past-president of Weston Advertising, Manchester, NH, March 4, 1990.
2. Personal interview with Dan Payne, Political consultant, Boston, February 6, 1990.
3. Neil Postman, *Amusing Ourselves to Death* (New York: Penguin Books, 1985), 61.
4. Interview with Weston.
5. Interview with Richard Ducey, Vice-president for Research, National Association of Broadcasters, Washington, D.C., February 14, 1990.
6. Judy Keen, "Big Chunks Go to TV," *USA Today*, February 2, 1988.
7. Joel L. Swerdlow, ed., *Media Technology and the Vote: A Source Book* (Washington, D.C.: Annenberg Washington Program, 1988), 83–84.

8. "Radio's Impact on Local Elections," *Info-Pak*, Washington, D.C., National Association of Broadcasters, March-April 1988.

9. Personal interview with Ken Swope, Ken Swope and Associates, Boston, January 25, 1990.

10. Interview with Payne.

11. Swerdlow, *Media Technology and the Vote*, 26.

12. Robert Hilliard, *Television Station Operations* (Stoneham, MA: Focal Press, a division of Butterworth, 1989), 65.

13. Swerdlow, *Media Technology and the Vote*, 9.

14. Interview with Payne.

15. Ibid

16. *Beyond the Thirty-Second Spot: Enhancing the Media's Role in Congressional Campaigns* (Washington, D.C.; Center for Responsive Politics, 1988), 14.

17. Leavitt J. Pope, president and CEO, WPIX, Inc., "Testimony before the Senate Communications Subcommittee on Lowest Unit Charge" given for the National Association of Broadcasters on his capacity as a member of the Television Board of Directors of NAB, Washington, D.C., August 2, 1989.

18. National Association of Broadcasters, Aristotle Industries, *Channels,* February 1988.

19. Pope, NAB testimony, p. 3.

20. Personal interview with State Representative Diane Wray Williams , St. Paul, MN, February 20, 1990.

21. Anne Rawley Saldich, *Electronic Democracy: Television's Impact on the American Political Process* (New York: Praeger, 1979), 40.

22. *Beyond the 30-Second Spot*, p. 22 Media data from the firm of Smith and Harroff.

23. Common Cause, Washington, D.C.

24. Jay Arnold, FCC Audit of Radio, TV advertising finds candidates often overcharged. *Boston Globe*, Boston, September 8, 1990, p. 3.

25. Interview with Payne.

26. Postman, *Amusing Ourselves to Death*, p. 46.

27. Personal interview with Dr. Robert Manoff, Co-Director, Center for War, Peace, and the News Media, School of Journalism, New York University, New York, February 12, 1990.

28. Interview with Swope.

29. Interview with Payne

30. Interview with Weston.

31. John O'Toole, President, American Association of Advertising Agencies, quoted in *Advertising Age*, November 28, 1988, p.17.

32. "The Role of Broadcasters in the Political Election Process," NAB White Paper, Washington, D.C.: National Association of Broadcasters, Adopted by the Board of Directors, January 17, 1986, p. 3.

33. Pope, "Testimony."

34. Interview with Swope.

35. Ibid.

36. Interview with Payne.

37. Ibid.

38. Interview with Swope.

39. Interview with Payne.

Issue Elections

FROM REPRESENTATIVE
TO DIRECT DEMOCRACY

Probably the most dynamic change in American democracy in the last half century rests not with candidates, but with the growing number of voter-initiated propositions on state and local ballots—a move toward using direct democracy to replace representative democracy in situations where the public lacks confidence in its representatives.

As is frequently the case with new trends in any society, the phenomenon is neglected by the mainstream—in this case neither political science texts nor broadcasters planning election coverage have thought much about this type of election. Each of us, whether in our role as broadcaster or as citizen, is affected by the laws regulating such things as health care, education, taxes, and civil rights. In recent decades these and many other issues have been decided by direct democracy—an election issue where the choice is up to the voter.

History of Initiative Petitions and Referenda

Rights of initiative petition and referendum as "tools of democracy" had only a few successes in the first half of the century, most notably the abolition of the bicameral Legislature in Nebraska in 1934. Between 1910 and 1968 less than 20 referenda questions had appeared on ballots in the United States. In 1968 a Sacramento auto dealer, Ed Koupal, launched a campaign to recall Governor Ronald Reagan. Direct democracy turned a new page in the history books. Between 1968 and 1980 about 60 ballot questions were put before American voters.[1] In the first half of the century, one ballot issue appeared on an average of every three years. In the last decade, five, on average, have appeared on the ballot each year.

Since the mid-1980s initiative petitions or referenda questions can be legally placed on the ballot in 23 states. In other states where it is not allowed at a state level, counties and municipalities do hold initiative petition elections. The trend is for more states to amend their state constitutions to permit this form of direct democracy—especially as disenchantment grows about conventional politicians.

Types of Elections

Initiative and referenda elections propose new state laws, new municipal ordinances, amendments to state constitutions, or municipal charters to be enacted or rejected by popular vote. In some cases, they are nonbinding votes taken to "send a message" to one's elected local or state legislative body.[2] They are defined as follows:

1. An *initiative* is enacting a law or constitutional amendment placed on the ballot by citizen petition (not through customary state legislature procedures);
2. A *referendum* is approval or rejection of a law or constitutional amendment passed by the legislature and placed on the ballot either by citizen petition or by the legislature;
3. A *recall* is a vote on removing an elected official from office in a special election called by citizen petition;
4. An *indirect initiative* is one that goes to state legislature on its way to the ballot box and it is not placed on the ballot if legislature votes to make it a law first;
5. An *advisory issue* has no force of law but is an expression of voter views on a given topic.

Each state or community has its own laws concerning the number of signatures required to place a question on the ballot and the deadlines for that activity. Broadcasters can update themselves by calling the Secretary of State's office, or, if appropriate, the county or local Election Commission.

Examples

Examples of referenda issues include: Colorado—an increased mineral severance tax, and a question regarding allowing grocers to sell wine; Florida—creating a state lottery; Nevada—a constitutional amendment to lower the state sales tax; Ohio—requiring popular election for public utility commissioners; Nebraska—banning corporate acquisition of farm land; California—a "bottle bill" that requires deposit and return for beverage containers. Other referenda items included issues such as requirements to shelter D.C.'s homeless, and in 1982, voters in ten states, 37 cities and counties, and the District of Columbia voted on the nuclear freeze referenda, the closest we've come to a national referenda. The tax-cutting referenda such as California's "Proposition 13" and Massachusetts' "Proposition 2½" have clearly had an impact on public policy. "Motor Voter" laws allowing people to register to vote when they renew their driver's licenses have passed in several western states and are gaining nationwide visibility.[3]

Future Influence

David Schmidt, Director of the Initiative Resource Center, observes that "where there's no initiative, it's a lobbyist's game, people feel they don't have influence."[4] The National Association of Broadcasters does not track the coverage given to issue elections because it is generally agreed that this facet of politics is a very small piece of the whole.[5] However, because technology is making it easier and easier for voter feedback, we can expect that this exercise of direct democracy will grow in the twenty-first century. The issue is how broadcasters can best cover this form of election. Various approaches are possible, including PSAs, free time for spokespersons on either side of the issue, feature programs, debates, and news coverage.

COVERAGE OPTIONS

PSAs

Ads for issue elections differ from candidate election ads in that they are not eligible for lowest unit cost. These ads should not, however, be grouped with commercial ads selling a product. Because of the importance of a ballot issue to the general public, these issue campaign ads deserve air time at the lowest unit cost. Issue election ads also differ from regular public service announcements in that they call upon the listener to make a decision at the ballot box. For example, the ad below was used in the 1982 Nuclear Weapons Freeze Referendum where voters in many states and localities across the U.S. were asked their position on requesting that United States and U.S.S.R. officials agree to freeze escalation of the nuclear arms race.

It is important to remember that while issue campaign ads ask for the listener/viewer to make a decision at the *ballot box*, they are like other PSAs in that they are raising an issue of public well-being for evaluation and decision. As "direct democracy" referendum campaigns grow in popularity, broadcasters will want to develop a policy regarding how the station will inform the public on both sides of a ballot issue. As with candidate elections, developing a policy and plan will serve the station better than relying on "ad hoc-ery" and the time consumed in resolving the resulting controversies.

The broadcasting industry has good background for thinking about issue election coverage because of the ever-increasing attention the industry gives to providing a range of public service messages and campaigns. These PSAs are simply industry's contribution to upgrading community well-being. A March 1988 NAB survey illustrates the scope of these public service activities: 75% of radio stations and 85% of television stations broadcast PSAs concerning AIDS during the previous month and over half the stations also aired AIDS-related news stories; 89% of the radio stations and 92% of television stations aired alcohol and drunk driving PSAs and over half the stations ran news stories on the topic; 90% of the radio and 95% of the television stations broadcast drug-abuse PSAs and over half aired local news stories on the topic. Half the stations provided PSAs on the dangers of cigarettes, and 20% are accepting condom advertising.[6]

:30 TV "Ballot Box"

MAN WITH BLOW-UPS OF WEAPONS . . . AND A BALLOT BOX:
There are a lot of ways to start a nuclear war and end life as we know it. Out of panic, stupidity, blindness, confusion. Or even by accident, the sort of computer error that's put our forces on red alert several times in the last few years. So many ways to start a nuclear war . . . and one good way to help stop it. The Nuclear Freeze is on your ballot this November.

SUPER: Vote for the Nuclear Freeze.

▶ *Figure 8   Issue Election PSA. Script prepared by Public Media Center, San Francisco, CA for national distribution by Nuclear Weapons Freeze Campaign.*

Free Time

Like a candidate campaign, and unlike the nonpolitical public service activities described above, an initiative or referenda campaign has a definite lifespan. In a few months, it's over. That makes it easier to cover as an event rather than an idea, as a race. Unlike candidate campaigns, a referenda or initiative campaign can easily be more than "talking heads." Because it focuses on some specific issue, good visuals are available for the enterprising investigative reporter.

As with the candidate campaign, the station could benefit by holding some planning sessions 6 to 9 months before the election, depending on the local political calendar, and planning a coverage strategy. This will allow time to accommodate full and fair coverage for all sides of the issue, time for appropriate investigative research, and time for making format choices that can increase both the public awareness of the choices and increase the audience satisfaction with the station's local news programming.

Format options generally remain the same as for candidate elections (see Chapters 3 and 4). Two exceptions exist. One is that "free-speech messages," including broadcast editorials and rebuttals, are an option in issue elections. Similarly, feature programming on the issue is also an option.

Other Public Service Activity

Many stations go beyond the PSA in their support of public service activity. For example, in 1986, the Illinois Broadcasters Association joined forces with the American Heart Association to involve 12 stations in a "Turn on Heart Radiothon." They recruited volunteers, did PSAs, held call-in programs, and interviewed doctors. This type of public service coverage is a separate and additional category to the public service that encourages the well-being of a system of self-government.

A major broadcast effort focused on the democratic process is the "Vote America Campaign" sponsored by the National Association of Broadcasters in cooperation with a number of national public interest organizations. The NAB is a clearinghouse for the spots and makes tapes available to local stations who add their own tag line. In addition, local stations often sponsor community-based "Get Out the Vote" events. In a March 1988 NAB survey, 94% of radio stations and 89% of television stations indicated that they planned to air PSAs to encourage voting.[7]

Even with this special broadcasting service, initiative and referenda issues have a tendency to fall between the cracks. In the traditional sense, they aren't news and they aren't elections, even though they are critical to the discourse that keeps democracy alive. Referenda can generate that excitement, it can empower the voter to keep the politicians accountable.

CONTROVERSY AND STATION POLICY

A referenda campaign advertisement will be a paid ad, not a donated PSA, and it does not fall under the "lowest unit rate" prices required for candidate campaigns. A station can decide whether or not to accept the ad, unlike a candidate campaign where the station is required to make time available.

Frequently, issue elections deal with controversial subjects. The broadcaster must decide how to handle controversial matter. A range of reactions can be documented. How can I take the ad when I vehemently disagree with its sponsor? If I take the ad it might "pollute" the buying atmosphere, making it impossible for the detergent advertiser to get his money's worth when the viewer is upset over the previous ad about nuclear war or abortion? If the ad displeases my listeners/viewers, how can I be sure I won't lose my audience?

For example, one ad produced by media consultant Ken Swope promotes improved commitment to education. It was sponsored by the Massachusetts Teachers Association. Street crime was a headline issue in Boston during this period, as was the role of Manuel Noriega in international drug trafficking. The ad focused in on kids shooting drugs on the streets and playgrounds. It implied that they were avoiding school. It then focused on a full-face picture of the former Panamanian leader and international drug dealer. The voice-over stated that Noriega would be delighted to see America's youth bypass the opportunity for education.

One local channel refused to air it, saying it was too controversial. Then, the same month, the station accepted an ad from the National Rifle Association encouraging women to own guns.

Each of these messages expressed a point of view—one, that educating youth reduces drug reliance and strengthens the country's stand against international trafficking—the other, that owning a gun is the way for a woman to be safe from crime. As individuals, each of us is entitled to agree or disagree with a given message. But, as broadcasters, to not cover an issue campaign is to "black out" the democratic process. Are there solutions that will enable the broadcaster to cover controversial issues without risking loss of business? One alternative is to establish a station policy to carry advertisements as purchased with a disclaimer both preceding and following each ad, something like "While this station supports free speech and the right to know about upcoming ballot issues, station coverage does not imply endorsement."

One problem in issue elections, as in candidate elections, is the tension between the right to hear all sides of an issue and the wealth or poverty of advocates to "get their message out." When the station develops its coverage policies, personnel might give consideration to how equity can be served in this situation.

Just as with PSAs, a station might consider establishing some policies for issue campaign advertising. Sample guidelines might include the following:

1. Be flexible in accepting spots of any length from 10 seconds to 2 minutes;
2. Provide candidates the option of submitting pre-recorded spots or having the station record the spot for a moderate fee assuming that the script, the voices, and the visuals are all prearranged by the candidate;
3. Make known in advance the standards the station sets for quality of voice and video;
4. Make clear the terms and policies for use of the broadcast facilities for those producing spots;
5. If a candidate provides a prerecorded spot, make clear in advance whether the system requires a presubmitted script and/or a storyboard;
6. State the station's policy for determining when a spot will be aired during a given calendar period;
7. State the station's policy concerning organizational identification on a tag line;

8. State the station's policy and procedures for coverage of both sides of highly controversial issues;
9. State the procedures and deadlines for submission of the ad and securing the placement and payment agreement.

Notes

1. David D. Schmidt, *Citizen Lawmakers: The Ballot Initiative Revolution* (Philadelphia: Temple University Press, 1989).
2. David D, Schmidt, ed., *The Initiative News Report*, Washington, D.C.: Initiative News Service, Roger Telschow and John Forster, publishers.
3. *Initiative News Report*, 3, no. 15 (July 1982). Also see "Initiative and Referendum: The Power of the People," Initiative Resource Center, Berkeley, CA. (Spring 1989).
4. Bart Asato, "Initiative Advocate Says Politicians Are Biggest Opponents, *"Honolulu Sunday Star Bulletin and Advertiser,"* January 24, 1988.
5. Personal interview with Dr. Richard Ducey, Director of Research and Planning, National Association of Broadcasters, February 14, 1990.
6. "Broadcasters Public Service Activities," *Info-Pak,* Washington, D.C., National Association of Broadcasters, May-June 1988.
7. Ibid.

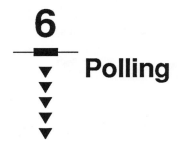

6

▼ Polling

A SNAPSHOT—NOT A VIDEOTAPE

Polling has become very important in informing the public of what selected samples of the public are thinking. Poll results are considered "hard news" and are used by broadcasters to make station policy decisions. In addition to independent polling, candidates rely on their own pollsters to determine public attitudes that help them map appropriate campaign strategies.

Broadcasters must constantly remind themselves and their audiences that although a poll can provide a good assessment of a point in time for a select sample of people, simply reporting "raw scores"—surface results—can be misleading. Fairminded broadcasters need to inform their audiences who was interviewed, as well as when and how the questions were worded. Before giving conclusions of reports, they need to remember that sampling error is less likely to be a problem than wording and context errors.[1] "Public opinion polls are subject to interpretation. Polls require explanations. Reporters simply do not transmit information about public opinion—they take an active role in interpreting and assessing it."[2]

A National Association of Broadcasters report warns:

The main difference between journalists and social scientists is that social scientists tend to use more rigorous methodologies. The science of survey research or polling is primarily in its methodology. Likewise, the art of survey research lies in the interpretation of results. Journalists should distinguish scientific from non-scientific polls and carefully interpret results in light of the particular methods used in the study.[3]

WHAT CAN SKEW POLL RESULTS?

No response, "don't know" answers, biases in sample selection, interpretations of answers by those who pay for the poll and those who conduct it, question phrasing, limits of options for response, ambiguity of response categories, and interviewer approach all bias poll results.

The sample selection will affect results. For example, polls of registered voters may not give an accurate indication of election trends in a situation where changing voter registration may swing that election. Subtle judgments enter into how questions are asked. For example, if asked who you prefer for "congress*man*", many respondents are subconsciously not likely to list a woman candidate. Timing of a poll also affects validity. There are fundamental problems in using early polls to prioritize station coverage. "Experienced pollsters know that an early strong or weak showing is often more apparent than real."[4]

Candidates try to use early polling for their own benefit where possible; considerable money is spent on early advertising in order to secure the high name-recognition that results in high ranking in early polls. The result is that the voters/audience is told by the broadcaster who the leading candidates are based on who has spent the money to buy name recognition. This exercise provides neither news about the actual campaigns nor substantive information about the candidates. Basically, the broadcasters are being used by the pollsters and the wealthier candidates.

A candidate's wealth can skew poll results. "One test of viability would be whether money could be raised, and that's determined pretty much by whether you can turn up in the polls at all, and THAT, in turn, is determined by whether you can get any visibility at all on television."[5]

This vicious circle can distort the campaign process, resulting in several problems: a) the public is not provided information to differentiate between wealth and credentials, b) the candidates who are not wealthy are not given equal opportunity, and c) the broadcasters, manipulated by the situation, lose their right to provide independent coverage.

POLLING USES

Uses by Broadcasters

News correspondents make many judgments in reporting poll results. For example, the poll is usually a "stop action" moment in time, not necessarily reflecting changes and trends. It may not include all the legally qualified candidates. There may be confusion about whether what is reported is absolute support for one candidate or the differences in support among candidates. Data are presented without explanation. Journalists can enhance or undermine the credibility of poll findings. "Journalists use polls to eliminate candidates with apparently little chance of winning a primary." Subtle differences in polling techniques can distort results.[6]

Evaluating candidate potential   Polls, "although they are largely untested indications of voter sentiment, they are the most common bases for evaluating a candidate's potential."[7] Broadcasters frequently use poll results to determine who to cover and who not to cover, or how to rank candidates in "tiers." The result is that some candidates are excluded from the election before the voting public has any chance to deal with it.[8] Chuck Crouse, political reporter for WEEI Radio, Boston, has editorialized:

> We [reporters] tend to get into ruts, covering candidates when they declare, pull out, win or lose. We call for discussion of the issues, but tend to skip covering issues as too boring . . .. There's no ideal answer to the question of how to cover a large field of candidates, but walking away from a candidate who doesn't conform to our expectations or rationing coverage on the basis of poll rankings falls well short of that elusive goal called fairness.[9]

Political media consultant Dan Payne says, "Stations who say that you can't cover all the candidates because the viewers won't watch those candidates they dislike can be carried to an extreme encouraging coverage only of the news that people like. We all know this is the opposite of what happens. News regularly covers crime, accidents, scandals, taxes—the stuff people don't like or are frightened of."[10]

Issue identification   Station polling often is used to identify the issues that candidates will debate. This selection process is very different from the one used to determine candidate popularity. In the situation of issue identification, the station needs simply to identify the range of concerns that interest the audience. There is no need for the precautions taken with candidate polls—because no one will ever vote on prioritizing all the issues. The poll simply identifies a range of topics appropriate for candidate debate.

Election night profiles   This polling data simply provides the audience with interesting information concerning the cross-section of persons who voted. No audience action is expected.

Election night projections   Projections of winners and losers is also no problem—if it is done after the polls close, when the information can in no way bias a voter response. In 1990 ABC, CBS, NBC, and CNN agreed to create a single exit poll, called Voter Research and Surveys, for election days in order to cut costs, and avoid the competition that has resulted in predictions of winners before the polls are closed.[11] This agreement came after many years of concern that announcing results on the East Coast before the polls close in other time zones could either cause voters to stay home or switch their vote.

Preserving the station image of impartiality   Polls claim to be impartial. But if the poll questions are skewed, or the results are reported with inappropriate selectivity, or the poll actually preempts the voters options, bias results.

Use of the Polls by Candidates
Polling has gained a biblical importance among candidates. In many cases, pollsters are no longer local firms. If a candidate wants PAC money, she is expected to use one of the half dozen or so national firms considered acceptable by the electioneering fraternity.[12] "It used to be that campaigns would go to their media person and ask for strategy. Now they ask their pollster. The pollster translates those numbers into the strategic recommendations that identify who your vote should be, what is of greatest concern to those who should be voting for you, and how you can best influence those groups."[13]

POLLING CONSEQUENCES

Interpretations
Interpretations of polling lead reporters to place value judgments on their stories. Language used includes phrases like "winner or loser," "front runner," "better than expected," "also running." One example of such value judgments was the report

that Eugene McCarthy won a "moral victory" because he came in a closer second than the pundits had predicted in the New Hampshire primary in 1968.[14]

While one might argue that only the voters have the right to narrow the field on primary election day, the press frequently does so, calls it that, and decides on the "viability," whatever that is, of various candidates. Rather than slip into this practice, broadcasters should take special care to report polls in context, that is, when it was made, who the sample included, and so on. In addition, broadcasters must take care not to draw definitive conclusions from any given poll.

Pack Journalism

Coverage of elections and polling results exercise a subtle influence on each other. Pack journalism is the tendency of journalists to cover what their colleagues cover. For example, according to the *Washington Post*, the coverage of the 1988 process of choosing a party nominee wasn't exactly equal time. There were 105 stories on the securing of the 85 delegate votes in Iowa. While 80 stories covered securing 40 delegates in New Hampshire, 53 covered the selection of the 2056 delegates on Super Tuesday. The problem is that a gut-feeling decision is made about when coverage is exciting and when it is "old hat." The public is led to believe that Iowa's 85 delegates are at least as important as Super Tuesday's multistate election of 2,056 delegates. The election coverage becomes distorted; the public and the broadcaster can lose sight of the fact that in the final count all votes carry equal weight. Pack journalism gives more credibility to hype than to the democratic process.[15] The same problem can occur on a local scale when more coverage is given to certain kinds of events than to other events.

UNSCIENTIFIC "POLLING"—900 NUMBERS

The advent of "900 numbers" has sparked the imagination of many broadcasters. This is the opportunity for a station to secure a 900 area code telephone number, where an audience can, for a small fee, call and register their opinion on a program, a candidate, or an issue. "Broadcasters think it is a creative way to stimulate interest in a program."[16] They are right. And the opportunity to talk back is certainly to be encouraged in a democratic society. However, in reporting the results, broadcasters must make very clear that the "poll" is not scientific—it reflects only those listening or watching who bothered to respond, and those zealots who had all their friends call.

WINNING A POLICY-MAKER OR A HORSE RACE?

Action plays best. A campaign based on polling figures only becomes a horse race. The tendency of broadcasters to use polling figures this way is understandable because a horse race happens. An issue just "is." To cover the campaign from an issue perspective could be viewed as boring, as a static nonevent.[17] Polling has helped us enter the era of "horse race" politics, because polling provides the numbers, the benchmarks for alleged progress.

In the 1986 congressional campaigns, 537 (well over 40% of all) stories on networks focused on the horse race, 312 (29%) on issues of the campaign, and 215

(20%) on issues of policy.[18] In the 1988 presidential campaign, networks broadcast 1,800 assessments of the candidates, only 200 or 10% of which were on issues, that is positions on policy or general ideology.[19] "Election coverage is less concerned with measuring the candidates qualifications for the job than with predicting their chance of winning it."[20]

Within the horse-race coverage, there are four types of stories:

1. The organizational and financial base of support for this candidates cam paign—10% of the stories;-
2. An indication of public support based not on actual voting but on polls—24% of stories;
3. Each candidate's electoral performance—10% of stories;
4. The subjective prognostication of pundits and analysts commenting on past performance and future expectations—56% of stories.[21]

Arbitrary horse-race coverage results in television bestowing momentum on some candidates and withholding it from others. Horse race broadcasting forces the candidates into a mold whereby timely trivia matters much more than issues.[22] Voters know little about a candidate's viability, or about what a candidate stands for. Mostly, they know who's ahead.[23]

Rather than fall into the horse-race coverage trap that results in limited, misleading, and superficial coverage of the election, take the sports analogy to its appropriate conclusion. Good sportscasting does not simply report who's ahead. It offers information on the criteria for evaluating excellence, the past performance of each competitor, the handicaps, for example, Chapter 4 offers a number of suggestions for appropriately covering the competition.

ACCURATE REPORTING OF POLL RESULTS

Richard Ducey, Director of Research and Planning for the National Association of Broadcasters states that "the evaluation, interpretation, and reporting of poll results is a very tricky business. Misstatements or misrepresentations of the data, deliberate or otherwise, can be damning to a news organization's credibility."[24] G. Cleveland Wilhoit and David H. Weaver's *Newsroom Guide to Polls and Surveys*[25] offers a number of points journalists should consider and, hopefully, share with their audience:

1. Who sponsored [paid for] the poll and who conducted it?
2. What were the actual questions asked, including the response choices offered the persons answering? [We strongly urge that the actual wording of the key questions be included in the news story.]
3. What was the population [or universe] which was sampled?
4. Was a probability [random] sample used? [If not, don't generalize to a larger group of people.]
5. What was the size of the total sample? Of subsamples or specific groups [such as registered voters] analyzed in the poll results?
6. If a probability sample was drawn, what is the estimated sampling error for the total sample? For any subsamples or specific groups?

7. What was the completion rate [response rate]? How many persons were interviewed from the total sample?

8. What results, if any, are based only on part of the total sample?

9. Was any weighting technique used to make the sample more representative of the population? [Note: This is a fairly common practice among survey researchers and does not imply anything "wrong" with the data.]

10. Are there any data available on population characteristics to compare with sample characteristics [such as percentages of blacks, males, females, registered Democrats, etc.]? Was such a comparison done?

11. How were the interviews done? [Face to face in the respondent's home, by telephone from a central business location, by mail, etc.]

12. When were the interviews done? What was happening at the time of the interviewing that might have influenced people's answers?

13. Could you as a journalist answer the questions in the survey? Were the questions clear and unambiguous?

14. What do other polls on the same subject say?

15. What was the purpose of the survey or the poll? Who is going to use the results for what purpose?

16. What else was found? Is the poll sponsor releasing data selectively, avoiding disclosure of less flattering results from other questions?

"VICTORIES"

If, after reading all the do's and don'ts of polling, your head is reeling, you might resort to humor as an acceptable form of election coverage. *Boston Globe* columnist Alan Lupo captured the election season in his "OpEd," paraphrased below:

They (the candidates) all start out promising they will discuss the "issues."—The candidates try to stick to their word—this does not last long for the following reasons:

1. The people aren't listening.

2. Neither are the media.

After awhile, it becomes clear that Candidate A, for whatever reason, is in the "lead." Candidate B is considered A's major threat. Candidate C is dismissed out of hand by the media.

A tries to avoid both B and C. C tries to get attention, but no one pays attention. B goes on the "offensive"—offensively. A wins, as predicted. B says A is great. A says B is great. If all this malarkey leaves you confused—next time vote for C.[26]

The challenge to the broadcaster is to make clear to the audience/voter the credentials of A,B, and C so that there is at least an opportunity for government to be led by the best qualified individual.

Notes

1. Personal interview with Dr. Richard Ducey, Director of Research and Planning, National Association of Broadcasters, Washington, D.C., February 14,1990.

2. William C. Adams, ed., *Television Coverage of the 1980 Presidential Campaign* (Norwood, N.J.: Ablex, 1983), 33.

3. Richard V. Ducey, "Public Opinion Polling as a Newsroom Source," National Association of Broadcasters, Washington, D.C., February 1984.

4. Stephen A. Salmore, and Barbara G. Salmore, *Candidates, Parties and Campaigns: Electoral Parties in America* (Washington, D.C.: Congressional Quarterly Press, 1985), 122

5. Marty Linsky, *Television and the Presidential Elections* (Lexington, MA: Lexington Books, 1983), Quote from Congressperson David Obey, (D-WI), 22.

6. Adams, *Television Coverage,* 34–40.

7. Robert S. Lichter, Daniel Amundson, and Richard Noyes, *The Video Campaign: Network Coverage of the 1988 Primaries* (Washington, D.C.: American Enterprise Institute for Public Policy Research, Center for Media and Public Affairs), 1989, 35.

8. Professor Henry Brady University of Chicago, lecture, "Does the Media Choose the President?" MIT Communications Forum, October 1987.

9. Chuck Crouse, reporter, Editorial WEEI Radio (CBS-affiliated all-news radio), Boston, June 2, 1987.

10. Personal interview with Dan Payne, political consultant, Boston, February 6, 1990.

11. "Network Accord on Poll Reported," *Boston Globe,* Boston, February, 25,1990, p. 8.

12. Personal interview with Merv Weston, President, Weston Advertising, Manchester, NH, March 4, 1990.

13. Salmore, Salmore, *Candidates, Parties and Campaigns,* 119.

14. Lichter, Amundson, and Noyes, *The Video Campaign,* 37.

15. Chris Krauthamner, "Media Scoreboard," *Washington Post,* February 19, 1988.

16. Interview with Ducey.

17. Salmore, Salmore, *Candidates, Parties and Campaigns,* 155.

18, Lichter, Amundson, and Noyes, *The Video Campaigns,* 14–15.

19. Ibid., 100.

20. Ibid., 33.

21. Ibid., 34–37.

22. Ibid., 106.

23. Brady lecture.

24. Ducey, "Public Opinion Polling," p. 2.

25. G. Cleveland Wilhoit and David H. Weaver, *Newsroom Guide to Polls and Surveys* (Washington, D.C.; American Newspaper Publishers Association, April, 1980), 78.

26. Alan Lupo, "The Truth about the Primary," *Boston Globe,* Boston, July 27, 1986.

7

The Technical Aspect

AMPLIFIED DEMOCRACY

Technological advance has created many additional opportunities for broadcasters interested in offering fair and equitable election coverage. Engineers, camera and sound crews, and editors are the spine of the system, making it possible for the story to be told. The equipment they use determines what kind of pictures can accompany a story, how those images look, what critical sounds are heard, how smoothly the story is edited, and how quickly the story can be transmitted to the listener/viewer, and how it is transmitted. Technological developments in communications have drastically changed democracy in the past 40 years.

The ancient Greeks considered democracy possible for the defined number of persons who could gather on a hillside at one time to see and hear a candidate, to debate the essential issues, and to vote. In 1948 Harry Truman campaigned 4000 miles by train. He met at most 1 million people. They cast their vote based on a speech, a handshake, and debating among themselves what was said and what they read. That was a whistle-stop campaign. In 1988 George Bush traveled a half mile in a boat in his opponent's backyard, proclaiming disgust for harbor pollution. He reached tens of millions. They cast their vote based on an electronic image and a personal evaluation of the message beneath the image. That was a media campaign.

TECHNOLOGICAL OPPORTUNITIES FOR ELECTION COVERAGE

SNG—Satellite News-Gathering

The first satellite network started in 1975 with Home Box Office (HBO). By 1984, KSTP-TV, in Minneapolis was pioneering satellite news-gathering (SNG) through a new system—the CONUS system created by their owners, Hubbard Communications. Prior to this, satellite news-gathering was reserved only for the networks. Today every local community can be live at important events. CONUS has revolutionized election coverage—especially state and national campaigns.

Hubbard Communications financed a transponder on a satellite on the KU band—14 Gigahertz. The higher the frequency, the shorter the antenna required, so for the first time a small truck with an 8 foot dish could provide SNG for a local station. Previously, satellite news required a flatbed truck with 18-foot dishes and equipment adequate for C Band transmission. Hubbard began to sell time to local stations across the continental United States. For example, for 5 minutes of satellite time a local station might pay less than $50.

WCVB-TV in Boston was the second station on the country to try CONUS. Jim Gilbert, WCVB's assistant chief engineer, recalls picking up the satellite news vehicle (SNV) in Tampa and driving to the Kansas City Reagan-Mondale debate at the height of the 1984 Presidential election campaign. "We pulled up next to the network flatbed trucks with their 18-foot dishes. They laughed at us. They were certain that the atmospheric conditions would make it impossible to transmit anything with so small an antenna. But our biggest problem was not the uncertainty of transmission, it was keeping easy access to a nearby pay phone. You see, back in 1984 there was no communication capability via the CONUS satellite. And there was no downlink ability to see what we were transmitting in our truck. So whenever we wanted to talk to the local station back in Boston, we had to hope we could reach them in time via pay phone. The first task after parking the truck was to locate a pay phone and mark it 'out of order' so we could have access to it when we needed it."[1]

Four years later, in 1988, Presidential candidates for the first time were able to campaign without traveling. A candidate could uplink a broadcast from one geographic location and be interviewed on the local news in as many locations across the United States as desired. For example, Rep. Richard Gephardt, candidate in the Democratic Presidential primary, sat in a rented TV studio in Austin, Texas, and appeared on the local evening news the same day with the local anchors in El Paso, Texas, Presque Isle, Maine, Augusta, Georgia and Tulsa, Oklahoma.[2]

A local station using SNG could apply the techniques used in Presidential races to U.S. Senate races, Governor's races, and in districts large enough to involve more than one media market, to U.S. House races. In Florida, for example, the Florida News Network joins together five cities in an uplink designed to cover statewide elections.

ENG—Electronic News-Gathering

In the 1970s microwave components on trucks up to 30 miles away made it possible to have portable news units. But the electronic news-gathering (ENG) made possible by computers and satellite services like CONUS revolutionized the local coverage of events away from the studio. It is possible to edit into a local broadcast any item of news immediately, and even to cover the local news from a location great distances from the station.

This technical capability has dramatically changed election coverage at every level. It has made it possible for viewers to have a live "presence" at events. It's a key factor in making local news a money-maker for local stations. With increased opportunities for local news comes increased opportunity for local election coverage: a function of keeping democracy alive.

But this potential expansion of democracy has also created some logistical problems. An example is the 1988 New Hampshire presidential primary. Eric Johnston, a video producer who worked as a sound technician during the primary describes the situation. "We had our own van and gear that ABC rented from our independent production company as part of the package sending us to New Hampshire for the last ten days before the election. Our hotel, just one of the sites, was surrounded with 40–50 trucks and satellite dishes, most of them from local stations. The League of Women Voters held a debate and it required an auditorium for the candidates and the audience, a gym full of news crews, each with their own lap top computer, and adjacent fields of trucks and satellite dishes. Then there are the camera and sound crews set up for covering debates, plus others let into the auditorium on a selective basis for "photo ops." You're set up in the auditorium waiting for the candidates to enter. The camera is adjusted. The sound is adjusted. Suddenly flashes and motor drives are all that's happening. The candidates have entered. But there certainly wasn't any audio you could get other than the camera sounds. There were many complaints about the numbers of crews, the limited space, and the pressure on crews not to miss anything. Increased media competition in such situations sometimes decreases civilized behavior. The same problem existed outside of formal events. You have one candidate talking with people. Beside her or him are a couple of assistants and the Secret Service. Twenty crews try to get the same shot. Each crew has a camera person shouldering a camera, and on the other end of an 8–10 foot cord a sound person carrying a deck, cables, tapes, and a pole mike. Everyone vies to get the best shot—the competition is intense."[3]

The mini-camera and other compact equipment available for ENG permit a reporter more flexibility and the opportunity to follow a candidate almost anywhere, obtaining pictures, information, and sometimes personal interviews not previously possible in large news gathering situations with the older bulky equipment. A newsperson might even leave a news conference and the moment it is over be prepared to catch the candidates in a hallway, an elevator, or in a parking lot.

Newsroom Computers

Taken for granted now, personal computers (PCs) appeared first in 1977. They have made possible dramatic changes in election coverage. For example, reporters have immediate access to the latest polling data, to constant downloading from the wire services at any terminal in the station, and access to any preprogrammed files on the candidates for a given race.

As with polling data (see Chapter 6), other information on races could be invaluable. For example, one could easily check a candidate's statement on an issue with his past public positions, past voting record on that issue, and with the special interests that might have contributed to that candidate's campaign. An investigative unit could store and update such data on each candidate and each race, making instant recall possible. Collaborative efforts could make it possible for stations to secure this material from their original source, like legislative records for voting history, or the Federal Election Commission for election contributors. This capability, if used to its fullest potential, can bring not only a new substance to the campaign coverage, but a new level of honesty to campaigning.

Computer Graphics

Character generators—typewriters that type on the TV screen rather than on paper—have been an essential part of listing program titles and credits for some time. But the marriage of computer and video has created new possibilities. Critical to preserving democracy in the age of television is making it possible to communicate substance about issues within the time and technology constraints of electronic media. Reading the 50-page issue paper is a thing of the past.

Computer graphics make it possible to communicate complex information in a picture form: a graph, a diagram, or an animation enables television to be substantive within the time and medium constraints. A graphics generator can break the monotony of "talking heads". A digital-effects generator can manipulate an image for creative and aesthetic purposes.

In the early 1980s the Quantel "Paint Box" revolutionized computer graphics. This data tablet and electronic pen enables the user to draw into the electronic memory a graphic that can be recalled on the air almost immediately. Prior to the Paint Box, one would have had to draw on paper the desired graphic, take a 35mm photograph of it, develop the slide, project the slide, and then air it.[4]

An example of computer graphics use was the series of animated graphics developed to explain to the viewer the Strategic Defense Initiative System (Star Wars) debated in Congress during the 1980s.[5] The animation explained in cartoon form the complex and controversial theory of deploying missiles that might actually attack, accurately hit, and destroy enemy missiles flying through outer space. The computer graphics can't totally explain the problems of accuracy at such distances and at such great speed, nor can it explain the problem of attacking decoys rather than enemy missiles; but computer graphics can accomplish a lot in demystifying a concept for the average viewer. Once aware of the situation, the viewer can then find the more detailed and specialized material.

Cable Television

Programming to specialized markets has increased dramatically. By 1995, it is projected that 75% of American homes will be wired for cable.[6] While not widely used yet for election coverage, cable's potential was recognized some years ago by Republican campaign consultant Richard Viguerie, and Howard Phillips, Director of the Conservative Caucus. They began considering the value of linking demographics research with narrowcast programming so that one could deliver one's message only to the particular voters one wanted to reach—for example, a largely blue-collar community, or a community with a high percentage of small children. Low cost, specialized audiences on local cable channels meet the requirements. An alternative approach for candidates to reach selected voters is to send each a videotape, possible now that VCR ownership is common.

Interactive Two-Way Communication Systems

Three examples of this technology are most applicable to broadcasting, providing full and fair election coverage and: 1) dedicated information retrieval systems; 2) personal computer–based interactive systems; 3) cable-based videotext systems.

Information Retrieval   One can subscribe to dedicated information retrieval systems. Two of the most noted ones for broadcasters are Lexis and Nexis. Lexis is a computerized legal database with access to citations, court cases, and a wide range of research on American, British, and French legal data. For election use this would be used principally in investigative research concerning a specific issue. Nexis, the system more useful for election coverage, is a news retrieval service. It draws on an information pool of over 100 newspapers, magazines, and specialized publications and allows one to do instantaneous research on a specific person, agency, or issue. News Net is a competing and similar electronic clipping service.[7]

Interactive Systems   PC-based interactive systems are distributed through telephone lines accesses via PC. *The Source* and *CompuServe* are examples of on-line data bases that provide information on news, tax codes, travel, and a host of topical issues (for example, the Olympics).[8] Material useful to the investigative reporter or to developing an in-house data base for an upcoming election might be obtained through this system in much less time than would ordinarily be required for research.

Cable Based Videotext   The first major experiment in videotex was "Qube," a two-way system launched in Columbus, Ohio in December 1977 that linked Warner Cable Company subscribers with the cable company's central computer through a keypad by the subscriber's set. The technology broadened the cable systems options in that a company could provide television programming, electronic transactions, and information and data bases.[9] Election applications can be extensive. One experiment asked subscribers to respond to a series of questions appearing on their screen after a speech by President Carter.

At present the Qube system has been abandoned due to an inability to make it profitable. But many other videotex services exist across the country. By linking television, computers, and telephones viewers can order newspapers, obtain specialized weather reports, subscribe to movies, and do their banking and shopping through videotex. For election use, a creative broadcaster could offer the closest link to direct democracy that has existed since the ancient Greeks gathered in the Agora—the marketplace. Viewers could be asked to respond directly to candidate comments and, ultimately, elections could occur electronically. We have not yet, however, reached the stage that guarantees the accuracy of single vote responses of the eligible voters in a given district.

TECHNICAL STAFF

It is important to understand the roles of the technical staff, with its direct impact on the reporting of elections.

The Editor's Job

As a rule, election coverage, like news, works against a deadline of air time. It's hard to always mesh quality products and speed. "Expediency is the enemy," according to WBZ-TV Boston's editor Terry Signaigo. The most important person working with the reporters to air a story is the editor. The reporter's story line and script determine the overall editing of the theme, sound-bites, and general visuals. An experienced and accurate editor knows best what it takes to get a piece ready to air on time.

Reporters may well not return to the station until shortly before air time. If they work in a market with vehicles containing tape-screening capability, they will have screened the material and written the story, but will not likely have edited it. Sometimes the reporter stays on the scene and microwaves the tape back for a writer to prepare the script for the on-air reporters. The reporter may include herself in the action of the taped report or may only include a voice-over narration. An editor constantly asks questions to help focus the exact sequence of the story, enabling the reporter to strengthen her idea with specific images and sequences.

Editing skills for election coverage differ from regular news. The average television news story is about 90 seconds in length. Sometimes time constraints prevent fair presentation of two sides of a story. The judgment call about what to include or exclude is made in the editing suite in cooperation with the reporter. However, in election coverage one is not just "reporting," one is making it possible for the voter/viewer to have full and fair coverage of all the legally qualified candidates and issues. To do otherwise is to preempt the opportunity for fair elections. Equal and fair coverage is an ethical essential, although most stations sacrifice that principle to expediency.

Minor changes that matter merely tighten the story or create better aesthetics in news reporting may be of major importance in election coverage. Edits can tilt the balance of fairness. The editor must be conscious of this when editing decisions are being made. Try not to provide more exposure to one candidate than another. Don't include some candidates' name placards and exclude others. Avoid featuring some campaign banners and omitting others. If today's piece cannot avoid a bias, correct it for tomorrow's piece.

Decisions about expediency, aesthetics, and simplicity for the audience must be made. To be fair to the election process, the only way to edit these stories is to make sure that equal video and voice time is given all candidates, or to show all candidates and use a reporter voice-over and computer graphics. In a large field, individual highlighting ought not to be done in news coverage, unless comparable attention can be devoted to the others in the field at a comparable time. In station sponsored events, such as debates, highlighting is easier because each candidate can be provided time for his message.

The Camera Crew's Job

Successful editing and full coverage opportunity depend in large part on how well the candidate's staff works with the camera crew. Better coverage of candidates is possible when the candidate's staff has someone who knows where the candidate is at any given time and is able to make her accessible for the photographer. Better coverage is possible when the candidate's staff and/or the hosts for an event provide a riser for the press, television lighting, and even a malt box (a multiple source audio deed from one microphone) for cleaner sound and easier audio, saving camera crews the trouble of fastening a dozen microphones to the podium. It helps to provide light behind the candidate, if appropriate, and to arrange the podium so that those who sit on the ends will fit into the picture.

As with reporting and editing, it is important for the photographer to remember that the ethical objective is not to get the most dramatic shots, not to focus on the most famous people, not to take what is easiest to shoot. The objective is to provide those who will see the tape with fair and equitable coverage of the field of candidates. Provide information for the audience's decision, not the reporter's. Media are accustomed to making such judgment calls in news and sports coverage; there are few models so far, however, for covering elections.

The most exciting photography in campaigns is not at the forum. The "run and gun" camera work commonplace to the early Presidential primaries serves as a model of applying new technologies to the coverage of the old-time "press the flesh" campaign trail. Reviving this direct voter contact campaigning might not be a bad idea. It can easily be done in local, county, and state elections. Because the technology encourages armchair campaigning with staged events, America's image of the candidate is the likeness on the screen rather than the real person in the neighborhood. Build time into a station election plan to send a camera crew out into neighborhoods to cover candidates discussing neighborhood issues. It will result in more exciting visuals than that offered by the staged event.

This live campaigning approach offers challenges for the camera crew. One ABC crew member from the 1988 New Hampshire presidential primary chronicled his experience as follows: "You're frequently walking backward down the street with the candidate in front of you. The camera person can't see anything other than what's in the lens of the camera. The sound person has to hold the mike in the right place while looking out for curbs, fences, cars, people, and other obstacles that might cause himself or the photographer to trip, lose the picture, and upstage the candidate. Ten days constantly running to cover the primary is a lot of work. If you're interested in politics, it's interesting to watch the campaigns develop. Meeting all the candidates and watching them deal with different situations is an exciting experience. But it's not just glitzy, it's work like any thing else."[10]

THE CHALLENGE AHEAD

The challenge ahead is to look systematically at the successes and failures of applying the new technology to election coverage, and to devise new models that can be used by broadcasters. The critics lament the artificiality of seeing candidates on the screen and the superficiality of brief stories and advertisements. Nonetheless, more voters have seen and heard the candidates than ever before in history. More voters have at least been exposed to the issues of campaigns than ever before. The challenge now is to focus the skills of broadcasters on the particular needs of election coverage, to develop viable election coverage plans, to establish ethical principles for fairness and objectivity in covering elections, and to explore the new possibilities for improved and more complete communication made possible by the new technologies.

Notes

1. Personal interview with James D. Gilbert, assistant chief engineer, WCVB-TV, Boston, March 8, 1990.
2. John Farrell, "Stumping Out, Media In as March 8 Nears," *Boston Globe*, February 29, 1988, p. 6.
3. Personal interview with Eric Johnston, freelance video producer, and sound technician who worked with the ABC news team at the 1988 New Hampshire primary, March 4, 1990.
4. Interview with Gilbert.

5. Michael M. Mirabito, and Barbara L. Morgenstern, *The New Communication Technologies* (Boston: Focal Press, 1990), 89–94.
6. Robert L. Hilliard, *Television Station Operations and Management* (Boston: Focal Press, 1989), p. 8.
7. Mirabito and Morgenstern, *New Communications Technologies*, 133.
8. Ibid.
9. Ibid, p. 136.
10. Interview with Johnston.

8

Government Systems
and Information Sources

INFORMATION ABOUT GOVERNMENT

To cover an election effectively, it is helpful to have some understanding about the jurisdiction of government, its major responsibilities, and to understand where one can find background information appropriate to asking intelligent questions. Reporters are frequently expected to be experts on everything. That expectation sometimes makes it difficult to ask important questions without seeming uninformed. The election reporter does have a number of discrete government sources for information and preparation.

Local Municipality and County Elections

The size of local jurisdictions varies from a few hundred voters to over a million. This level of government includes elections in towns, cities, counties, and a range of special regional entities from school committees to health agencies, to planning commissions to courts. Often these elections are nonpartisan, without the traditional Republican versus Democrat labels common on the state and national levels.

The Charter or By-Laws of a given jurisdiction will tell you which offices are elective, which are appointed by the elected official, and which are career civil service positions hired through an application procedure. The titles of offices and officials, the method of selecting them, and the principal legal document spelling out the powers of a jurisdiction differ from locality to locality. Start with a phone call to the secretary in the office of the local chief executive (Mayor, Selectperson, Manager, Commissioner, or other title). Ask where to obtain some of the publications identified below:

Charter;
By-laws;
Directory of elected and appointed officials (with terms of office);
Ordinances relevant to describing the job of key officials;
Budget for area the official oversees.

State Elections

Governing a state involves electing a number of officials designated in the state constitution, including the Governor and the state Legislature. The status of other officials such as Lieutenant Governor, Attorney General, Secretary of State, state

Treasurer, state Auditor, and others varies from state to state. A call to the secretary in the governor's office should help you identify which office to visit to find some of the documents listed below:

State *Constitution*;
General Laws pertaining to descriptions of key positions;
Budget for given area of government;
Executive Orders, rules, or other materials concerning operations procedure for said office.

Federal Elections

Article I, Section 1 of the U.S. Constitution vests all legislative powers in the two-house Congress. No bill can become law without passing both the House of Representatives and the Senate. Among the many powers enumerated in the Constitution, Congress may set and collect taxes, amend the Constitution, and declare war.

A Representative must be 25 years old and have been a citizen for 7 years. Members of the House of Representatives are elected every 2 years. The number each state has depends on the last U.S. Census. A congressional district is a jurisdiction with a population of approximately 500,000 persons. A Senator must be 30 years old, and have been a citizen for 9 years. Senators are elected every 6 years. Each state has two; their terms are staggered.

Article II, Section I, Clause 4 of the Constitution states that one must be a natural-born citizen at least 35 years old to serve as President or Vice-President. It provides the following job description: the President must be capable of being Commander-in-Chief of the military. The President "shall have the power, by and with the Advice and Consent of the Senate, to make Treaties, . . . shall appoint Ambassadors, other public Ministers and Consuls, Judges of the Supreme Court" and others.

To secure documents about federal government one might a) go to a local library, b) go to a federal government book store in the building where your regional federal offices are located, the largest city for your region of the country, c) write the U.S. Government Printing Office (GPO), Washington, D.C., d) call the office of the Congressperson for your district and ask someone on the staff to send you a listing of available GPO publications. Some of the documents you might want include:

The U.S. Constitution;
The "U.S. Budget in Brief" for the current fiscal year;
Congressional Staff Directory, P.O. 62 Mount Vernon, VA 22121, for a listing of who does elected official's key staff work, the AA, Administrative Aide, or the LA Legislative Aide.

Parties/Delegates/Conventions

Political parties are most visible at the national and state level. Their membership, however, is built from those who are elected in local ward and town elections, usually during the presidential primary elections. As a rule, it is these people who rise through the ranks and are elected as delegates to the nominating conventions for state officials, or elected to the state and national party committees to make the rules and facilitate the campaigns of those who later emerge as party nominee for president.

It has become common practice to provide media coverage of party conventions. That, as a rule, is not where the action is. In actual fact, the action is at the preconvention events such as caucuses that elect delegates prepledged to vote for certain candidates, and committee meetings of the party that determine the rules for convention procedure and determine the details of platform positions. By and large, by the time of the convention the disputes have been resolved and those with the power to emerge victorious have a predetermined script to follow. At a national level, the party determines, with state leadership, the sequence of presidential primaries, as well as the method for delegate selection and delegate vote counting at conventions. Although these committee meetings and preliminary caucuses are usually not newsworthy, these actions often contribute heavily to one person being nominated and another not. When a broadcaster covers such a preliminary activity, the audience should be told the larger significance of the event as well as who to contact if one wants to participate in this process.

At the national level the parties also focus efforts on ensuring that their nominee will win the popular vote in enough states to secure 270 of the 539 electoral votes needed to become president. The states that count are those with the largest numbers of electoral votes, that is, those with the largest populations and therefore the largest congressional delegations. A state's electoral votes equal its number of Congresspersons and Senators. Communication technologies have reduced parties' roles in terms of building the legendary ward machine for envelope stuffing, patronage, and reaching the voter. The traditional local approach has been largely replaced with media personality politics. Whether the old "machine" or new "media" approach is used, the bottom line for parties is winning the right number of votes in the right places.

Primaries/Caucuses/General Elections

The choices available to the voters in the general election—at local, state and national levels—depends on the choices made at the time of the primary election. Except for the few highly visible Presidential primaries, this level of election receives far less attention than it warrants. Similarly, because people don't understand the process and don't see that it will affect them personally, the primary voter turnout usually is very low. In recent years only about 20% of the nation's eligible voters have been responsible for electing the presidential nominees.

Participatory Democracy

Town meetings, such as those held in small communities in New England, and initiative petitions/referenda ballot items are a form of direct democracy. Chapter 6 covered these elections. The election laws are set down by the state or local jurisdiction and are important in that they identify the number of signatures and the deadlines for putting items on a ballot for popular vote.

WHERE TO GET DATA

Demographics

The U.S. Census Bureau and the U.S. Department of Labor's Bureau of Labor Statistics have local demographics, some of it updated from the last census. This material is available by contacting their nearest regional office. Your local government planning and development office probably has purchased the data for its jurisdiction and may have it both in print form and on computer disc. To avoid drowning in data, one might contact the state office responsible for planning or for liaison with municipalities and obtain a "monograph" on your community. In some places, your local government or your metropolitan regional planning agency may have aggregate data that provides enough information.

The research department of your station will also have data on the demographics of the station's market area, and it might prove interesting to compare this with government produced statistics. Remember, however, that the station's market area is probably not identical to the area for a particular election jurisdiction.

Voting Data

Election regulation and monitoring agencies exist at all three levels of government. For federal candidates, the Federal Election Commission (1-800-424-9530) can provide you with computer printouts of the campaign contributions to candidates running for Congress. Election return data is available through your local election commission. It can give you information on how many people are registered to vote in your jurisdiction, what the party registration count is, how many voted in past elections, and which candidates received how many votes in past elections. This material can be analyzed to determine that a given candidate's base of support comes from only one geographic part of the district. It can be correlated with census data to draw a demographic picture of what kind of people are likely to support which candidate.

State election oversight includes coordination with municipalities on all aspects of running elections. In addition, state government (either the Secretary of State's Office or the Attorney General's Office) will have legal staff able to interpret the legality of issues concerning such things as deadlines for referenda campaigns, wording on the ballot, candidate identifiers on the ballot, and minority party eligibility.

Incumbent Records

Government Finances   Each level of government is required to follow a prescribed process whereby the Executive annually presents a budget to the legislature for approval. These are public records. The budget, while sometimes difficult to understand, does at least provide a good directory of all the departments and offices in that level of government, and the costs of their operations. Note, however, that sometimes grant monies from other levels of government or private foundations, revenues from fees and licenses, and bond monies are not included in the principal budget document.

Government Decisions   A valuable reference for Congressional races is *The Almanac of American Politics*.[1] This book profiles your district, and identifies how the incumbent is ranked by various public interest groups on key issues.

Detailed records concerning members of Congress can be obtained from the Congressional Citizen Information Service for specifics (1-800-392-6090). At the state and local levels, election data is usually kept by the Secretary of State. The clerk of the Legislature or of the local Council has the records of votes on matters placed before the body. Information on other decisions made by elected or appointed state and local officials can be found in the Annual Report and in other files kept by state or local agencies. These are, with few exceptions, public records.

Internal Checks and Balances   Often one government office may produce reports that contradict another government office, either because its specialization is different or because it is charged with providing a critique of the other office. For example, the Congressional Budget Office serves to provide a check and balance review of the White House Budget Office. The General Accounting Office studies the work produced by other departments of government. The Congressional Research Service provides an independent research resource for the legislative branch of government.

For the public the Freedom of Information Act (FOIA), is the principal tool for securing government reference material. The U.S. Government Printing Office can provide you with a brochure describing how one files an FOIA request. Note, however, that under the Reagan administration more and more execptions were granted to federal agencies, allowing them to withhold information from the public. Almost any controversial matter can be kept confidential by classifying it as a national security matter, thus making it impossible for an investigative reporter to serve the public's right to know.

At a state and local office, resources within the legislative branch often are too small to provide adequate professional-level analysis of problems. When that is the case, the reporter can turn to the private sector as noted below under private and public interest organizations.

Public Institution Officers and Hierarchy

Every level of government publishes a directory of its officers, their terms of office, whether they are appointed or elected, and how to reach them. These directories are usually available from the Clerk's office in the respective jurisdictions. Another valuable reference document is the in-house telephone directory for a given government jurisdiction. This will give you the names of your most valuable contact persons, the key staff who work for the elected or appointed official.

Private and Public Interest Organizations

Spokespersons   Business and professional associations, universities, unions, private nonprofit public interest groups, political action committees, and a host of other organizations exist that do substantial professional research on various aspects of government involvement in certain issues. Local libraries will usually have directories of pertinent organizations and officials and are a good source of such information. Often it is necessary to contact several groups before you get all the information you might want.

Data—External Checks and Balances   Many of the public-interest nonprofit associations that are advocates for particular issues have access to well-researched materials on their particular interest. The secretary of state's list of nonprofit groups registered will provide the names of such groups if the telephone directory or your local library hasn't provided them. University libraries, appropriate university department chairs, libraries in major public interest organizations, and consultants who work in the field are other information sources. Computerized data services noted in Chapter 8 are other sources.

IDEAS ON ELECTION COVERAGE FROM OTHER DEMOCRACIES

While our principal concern is how to handle American election coverage within the framework of the American broadcasting industry, it's always useful to learn from others. In 17 of 21 democratic countries surveyed, broadcasters give free time to political parties to broadcast programs of their own design and production before elections. In some countries, such as Australia, Denmark, Finland, France, Japan, Netherlands, and Turkey, time is given equally to all parties. In others, such as Austria, Belgium, Canada, West Germany, Ireland, Italy, Spain, Sweden, Switzerland, and the United Kingdom, time is given proportional to party voting strength. Time is not given at all in India, Norway, and Sri Lanka.

Although such political broadcasts get respectable, although not top ratings in the countries where they are made available to the public, their most important contribution is to "give the politicians and the parties the chance to present themselves as they see themselves, not as passed through the newscasters filters and prisms.[2]

United Kingdom   In the general election, each major party is given five 10-minute television broadcasts sprinkled throughout the campaign. Lesser parties get fewer slots based on the percentage of vote they received in prior elections. Each segment is broadcast simultaneously on all channels to minimize "tune-out." The fact that the allocations were by party reminded the voters that the choice was not just personalities, but party ideology too.[3]

Finland   Finnish Broadcasting Company, a public system, has prescribed regulations stating that before parliamentary and municipal elections, and elections to chose presidential electors, special election programs will be broadcast where representatives of registered parties shall be heard. Each party has equal status on these programs regardless of its size (membership in Parliament). Most typical programs are interviews where one or two candidates from a given party are interviewed. Each party gets the same air time and the order of appearance is drawn by lots. Election debates involve representatives of each party on one program. All the allocated time is free to the candidates.[4]

Sweden   The broadcasting company is free of commercials, operated on a subscription basis. The law states that impartial coverage is essential, especially during the last 2 months of campaigning. During this period, discussions of incumbent activity must be accompanied with discussion of other viewpoints. The main election programs are five hearings (each 50 minutes long) to scrutinize each of the seven parties and its activity on such matters as the environment and energy, family policies, social welfare, taxes and the economy, law, and justice. In addition, two debates (each 2 hours and 20 minutes) occur involving all seven political parties. In September 1988, for example, one debate focused on the environment and the other on the economy. Finally, a few days before the election an "all-night" debate occurs among the five parties with incumbents in Parliament. These programs are usually rerun once or twice. Two special programs (1½ to 2 hours long) provide election programming for non-Swedish speaking immigrants and include debates on immigrantion policy.[5]

The Swedish broadcasting system may not mention nominated candidates except in connection with specified election programs, unless it is necessary in the context of reporting news and current events. This practice goes into effect after nominations for national offices and 1 month before the election for local officials.

Australia   According to the Australian Broadcasting Tribunal, the country's regulatory authority, there are no explicit provisions for free access. However, if one party is given access, then other parties must be given equal access. This does not apply to news coverage or to paid political advertising. Election coverage begins when the election is announced, usually 3 to 4 weeks before the day of the vote. There is a ban on political coverage and paid political ads during the last 3 days before the polls open.[6]

Denmark   The Danish Supreme Court has ruled that all political parties involved in an election must have equal access to radio and television, equal transmission time, equal question time, and equal debate time. The finer details are worked out in advance of each election by a committee of broadcasters and members of Parliament. The election period in Denmark is fairly short—3 to 4weeks.[7]

New Zealand   In 1990 the debate over free time dominated the New Zealand election coverage discussions. The government amended the Broadcast Act, tripling the amount of time broadcasters must provide free to major political parties. Before the amendment passed each of the country's three television networks provided 2 hours of free air time to each of the major parties. Now they must provide 200 minutes excluding time set aside for coverage of opening and closing addresses. Radio previously provided a total of 6 hours of free political advertising. Now the public stations must cover only the opening and closing statements, but the commercial stations must supply 150 minutes for political ads.[8]

KNOW YOUR WAY AROUND

The extent to which new broadcasters will need to know how government works depends on the specific nature of their jobs. One of many professional tracks is possible. Small local stations without much staff may provide the new employee an immediate chance to demonstrate skill by doing election coverage along with other station jobs. In larger stations, news directors usually oversee the election coverage planning, with the more seasoned producers and reporters responsible for coverage. The new broadcaster can learn from others and test her ideas and techniques on colleagues. Networks focus principally on covering presidential elections, with limited coverage of selected House, Senate, and governor's races. The magnitude of this job requires sophisticated management organization. A network might well have separate sections for each of the following: 1) investigative research; 2) polling—pre-election and exit polling; 3) statistical work critical to projecting election results; 4) an executive producer's staff to pull the overall package together and handle election night; and 5) a separate section for ongoing political coverage. New employees in networks might find their work highly specialized and mostly behind the scenes.

Notes

1. Michael Barone and Grant Ujifusa, *The Almanac of American Politics 1990* (Washington , D.C.: National Journal, 1989).
2. Austin Raoney, *Channels of Power: The Impact of Television on American Politics* (New York: Basic Books, 1983), 180.
3. Larry Sabato, "TV Politics: The Influence of Television in Political Campaigns," George Rodman, ed., *Mass Media Issues.* (New York: CUNY, Brooklyn College, 1984), 94.
4. Personal correspondence with Risto Volanen, Director of Planning, Finnish Broadcasting Company, Helsinki, Finland, March 6, 1990.
5. Personal correspondence with Anders Burholm, who translated materials from Stockholm Channel 2 officials, Stockholm, Sweden, March 5, 1990.
6. Australian Broadcasting Tribunal, N. Sydney, Australia. Also personal correspondence with Professor Peter White, Monash University, Clayton, Victoria, Australia.
7. Information from Dan Larsen, Denmark, with translation provided through personal correspondence with Jens Lund, Teaching for Peace Workshop, Arhus, Denmark.
8. Matthew Grainger, and Mike Munro, "[Prime Minister} Palmer Stands by Increase in Political Ads," *The Dominion*, Wellington, New Zealand, March 13, 1990. Also see Wendy Frew, "Outcry Forces Review of New Zealand Election Ads," *Financial Review*, Melbourne, Australia, April 3, 1990, p. 18.

9

▼ Election Laws
▼ and Regulations

THE AMERICAN ELECTION FRAMEWORK

Reference documents are available to broadcasters on both the Federal Communication Commission (FCC) and the Federal Election Commission (FEC) requirements for fair elections (see addresses in endnote[1]).

Broadcasters are most familiar with FCC regulations, especially Section 315 of the Communications Act of 1934, As Amended, which includes the Equal Time provision. Federal Election Commission regulations, while having less direct impact on the broadcaster, do provide excellent sources for election news coverage, such as periodic reports of the candidate's political committee, specific donors to a candidate's current campaign, donors to a past campaign, campaign finance laws, and practices that are considered illegal means of securing campaign support.

Federal laws and regulations covering broadcasting generally apply to candidates for nonfederal offices as well as those running in federal elections. Laws and regulations covering election qualifications and procedures can be found at federal, state, and local levels of government.

CANDIDATES FOR FEDERAL OFFICE

Federal Communications Commission Law

Relevant laws and regulations governing local stations for local and state elections, as well as federal elections, are in the Communications Act of 1934, As Amended, and as interpreted in *The Rules and Regulations of the Federal Communications Commission.*

A summary brochure on political broadcasting is published by the FCC at periodic intervals and is the most useful document for the practicing broadcaster.[2] It provides citations from relevant enforcement rulings and court cases to clarify interpretations of the law. This *Political Broadcast Handbook* and other publications are listed on page 97. Changes in detail as they occur can be monitored in the following publications:

Broadcasting, a weekly publication of Broadcasting Publications, Inc., Washington, D.C.

The Federal Register, a daily publication of the federal government listing all news related to changes in laws and regulations. It is available in major libraries.

The Code of Federal Regulations, Title 47, contains FCC actions. The most
recent edition can be obtained through the U.S. Government Printing Office,
Washington, D.C.

Within the FCC, the Mass Media Bureau and the Office of the General Counsel
have joint responsibility for rulings. For information or clarification of a given point,
write to The Fairness/Political Programming Branch, Mass Media Bureau, FCC,
Washington, D.C., 20554, or call 202-632-7586.

Highlights of FCC laws and regulations that the broadcaster and cablecaster
should know include:

Legally qualified candidate   Rule 73.1940 (a) states:

Any person who has publicly announced that he is a candidate for nomination by
a convention of a political party or for nomination or election in a primary,
special, or general election, municipal, county, state or national and who meets
the qualifications prescribed by the applicable laws to hold the office for which
he is a candidate, so that he may be voted for by the electorate directly or by
means of delegates or electors, and who: (1) has qualified for a place on the
ballot, or (2) is eligible under the applicable law to be voted for by sticker, by
writing in his name on the ballot, or by other method, and (i) has been duly
nominated by a political party which is commonly known and regarded as such,
or (ii) makes a substantial showing that he is a bona fide candidate for nomination or office, as the case may be.[3]

Equal Time   Section 315(a) of the Communications Act of 1934, As
Amended, states:

If any licensee shall permit any person who is a legally qualified candidate for
any public office to use a broadcasting station, he shall afford equal opportunities
to all other such candidates for that office in the use of such broadcasting station:
Provided, That such licensee shall have no power of censorship over the material
broadcast under the provisions of this section. No obligation is imposed under
this subsection upon any licensee to allow the use of its station by any such
candidate. Appearance by a legally qualified candidate on any (1) bona fide
newscast, (2) bona fide news interview, (3) bona fide news documentary (if the
appearance of the candidate is incidental to the presentation of the subject or
subjects covered by the news documentary), or (4) on-the-spot coverage of bona
fide news events (including but not limited to political conventions and activities
incidental thereto), shall not be deemed to be use of a broadcasting station within
the meaning of this subsection.[4]

"Reasonable Access" for All Candidates   Section 312(a) of the Communications Act of 1934 states:

(a) The Commission may revoke any station license or construction permit...(7)
for willful or repeated failure to allow reasonable access to or to permit purchase
of reasonable amounts of time for the use of a broadcasting station by a legally
qualified candidate for Federal elective office on behalf of his candidacy.[5] This

includes candidates running independently or on non-traditional party tickets. It also includes candidates who some believe have no chance to win.[6]

"Lowest Unit Advertising Rates"   Section 315(b)(1) of the Communications Act of 1934 as amended states:

> The charges made for the use of any broadcasting station by any person who is a legally qualified candidate for any public office in connection with his campaign for nomination for election, or election, to such office shall not exceed (1) during the forty-five days preceding the date of a primary or primary runoff election and during the sixty days preceding the date of a general or special election in which such person is a candidate, the lowest unit charge of the station for the same class and amount of time for the same period, and (2) at any other time, the charges made for comparable use of such station by other users thereof.[7]

Fairness Doctrine   The Fairness Doctrine essentially developed in 1949 and functioned as a regulation, until its demise in 1987. It was never codified as a law. Basically, it had two parts: the first requiring broadcasters to present controversial issues, the second requiring that when one side of a controversial issue is presented, an obligation exists to afford reasonable opportunity for the presentation of contrasting views. The Fairness Doctrine was highly controversial, strongly opposed by the broadcasting industry, and strongly supported by citizen groups and civic organizations. In the mid-1980s the Supreme Court said the FCC, not the courts, was empowered to enforce it since it wasn't a law. The FCC announced that the Fairness Doctrine was no longer operable. "In today's information marketplace, the Fairness Doctrine's excessive government intervention in the editorial process, and its documented chilling effect on constitutionally protected speech, compel us to conclude that it is no longer constitutional or in the public interest.... We support the laudable goal of fairness in the coverage of controversial issues of public importance be broadcast licensees."[8]

Shortly thereafter, Congress passed it as a law. President Reagan vetoed it. The Senate did not have sufficient votes to override the veto. It has not existed since 1987. But efforts to pass the law continue and it is included here because many stations continue to operate as if it were still policy, and there is some expectation that Congress will enact a fairness law in the early 1990s.

Some argue that the Fairness Doctrine hampered broadcasters First Amendment rights. Others argue that the Fairness Doctrine still stands since a 1969 unanimous Supreme Court upheld the Fairness Doctrine as constitutional. See the *Red Lion Broadcasting versus FCC case*.[9] While broadcasters argue that the Fairness Doctrine limited their freedom of speech, citizen groups argued that it expanded freedom of speech for more citizens and more points of view.

Public Access to Station Records   Broadcasters are required to keep "political file" records. Rule 73.1940(d):

> Every licensee shall keep and permit public inspection of a complete record of all requests for broadcast time made by or on behalf of candidates for public office,

together with an appropriate notation showing the disposition made by the licensee of such requests, and the charges made, if any, if request is granted. Such records shall be retained for a period of two years.[10]

Section 73.112(a) of the Commission Rules:

The following entries shall be made in the program log—(1)(v) An entry for each program presenting a political candidate, showing the name and political affiliation of such candidate.—(2)(iii) An entry showing that the appropriate announcement(s) (sponsorship, furnishing material or services, etc.) have been made as required by Section 317 of the Communications Act—(4)(ii) An entry for each announcement presenting a political candidate showing the name and political affiliation of such candidate.[11]

Broadcaster Editorials   Rule 73.1930 states:

Where a licensee, in an editorial, (1) endorses or (2) opposes a legally qualified candidate or candidates, the licensee shall, within 24 hours after the editorial, transmit to respectively (i) the other qualified candidate or candidates for the same office or (ii) the candidate opposed in the editorial, (a) notification of the date and time of the editorial; (b) a script or tape of the editorial; and (c) an offer of a reasonable opportunity for candidate or spokesman of the candidate to respond over the licensees facilities: Provided, however, that where such editorials are broadcast within 72 hours prior to the day of the election, the licensee shall comply with the provisions of this paragraph sufficiently far in advance of the broadcast to enable the candidate or candidates to have a reasonable opportunity to prepare a response and to present it in a timely fashion.[12]

Free Time   A key decision in providing free time for bona fide candidates, *Kennedy for President Committee versus FCC*, 636 F.2nd 432 [D.C. Cir. 1980] stipulates that if a station makes reasonable amounts of time available for purchase by federal candidates, it is not required to also provide them with free time. However, a 1983 ruling enabled stations to sponsor and candidates to participate in debates without violating the FEC prohibition on corporate contributions to candidates.

Federal Election Commission Laws

Federal Election Commission laws, regulations, and related state and local laws govern candidates. State laws determine how one qualifies as a candidate. A broadcaster must be familiar with the highlights of these laws and regulations and know where to get further information in order to broadcast the election accurately. The FEC publishes a brochure titled *Federal Election Campaign Laws* that highlights pertinent laws and regulations governing candidate campaign operations. This can be obtained by writing the Federal Election Commission, Washington, D.C., 20463 or by calling their toll free number 1-800-424-9530.

You can monitor ongoing changes in election requirements in the publications listed below:

Federal Register, published weekly and available in larger libraries.
Code of Federal Regulations, Title 11, which can be ordered from the U.S.
Government Printing Office or the FEC.

CANDIDATES FOR STATE OFFICE

States specify the reporting requirements, the dates for elections, and the campaign finance restrictions for candidates at all levels of government. At the state government level, the election oversight function is often located within the Secretary of State's office. If you are interested in materials for many states rather than just your own, the Federal Election Commission's National Clearinghouse on Election Administration in cooperation with the Congressional Research Service of the Library of Congress periodically issues a summary of regulations in all 50 states. This document is titled *Campaign Finance Law* and can be obtained from the FEC.

CANDIDATES FOR LOCAL OFFICE

Separate laws governing election practices are not likely to exist at this level, although local charters and ordinances can regulate who is elected, when, and where. The Clerk's office in any municipality can provide a copy of the municipal Charter and copies of local ordinances. The local government's Election Department will be the repository of all election records, including district maps, voter lists, party affiliations, certifications of legally qualified candidates, membership elected to local party organizations, authorized ballot language, order of ballot listing, and past election results. In some areas of the country, the county government offices would be the repository for this information.

Notes

1. For updated summaries of the applicable laws and regulations governing elections see the following:

   The Law of Public Broadcasting and Cablecasting: A Political Primer (Washington, D.C.: Federal Communications Commission). A brochure updated at periodic intervals.

   Federal Election Campaign Laws (Washington, D.C.: Federal Elections Commission). A brochure updated at periodic intervals.

   Political Broadcast Handbook, a legal guide for broadcasters, candidates and advertising agencies, is published at regular intervals by the National Association of Broadcasters and available in most stations. It focuses on FCC law, not FEC.

   Beyond the 30-Second Spot: Enhancing the Media's Role in Congressional Campaigns (Washington, D.C.: Center for Responsive Politics, 1988). This book reviews political broadcasting laws and discusses proposals for modification from the point of view of a research organization interested in elections but independent of both candidates and broadcasters.

   In addition, the election division of the secretary of state's office will have publications concerning the laws governing candidates running for state and local offices.

2. Ibid.
3. The Rules of the Federal Communications Commission. Note: for broadcasters the definition is found in Section 73.120; for cablecasters the definition is Rule 76.5.
4. FCC, Washington, D.C.
5. The Communication Acts of 1934, As Amended.
6. *The Law of Political Broadcasting and Cablecasting: A Political Primer*, (Washingrton, D.C.: Federal Communications Commission, 1984), 13–14.
7. The Federal Communications Act of 1934, As Amended.
8. *Memorandum Opinion and Order*, Federal Communications Commission, Washington, D.C., April 7, 1988. Also personal interview with Milt Gross, Chief, Equal Time Division, FCC, Washington, D.C., February 13, 1990.
9. "FCC's Repeal of Fairness Doctrine Survives Supreme Court," *Broadcasting*, January 15, 1990, pp. 56–57.
10. The Rules of the FCC governing radio broadcast services. Section 73.120 (d).
11. Rules of the FCC.
12. Ibid.

Conclusion

As a new century dawns, it is time for the best and the brightest in broadcasting to mesh high ratings, good profits, professional rewards, and campaign victories with the techniques for reporting elections that provide a renaissance for legitimate democracy.

To do so will not only fulfill the broadcasters' responsibility to the democratic process but will also improve the quality of the station's news coverage. When the job of reporting elections is well done, seven things will have been accomplished:

1. The voters/audience will know the description of the job to be filled—the criteria for excellence against which to measure each candidate for the job.
2. All the legally qualified candidates will be able to get their message broadcast—equally.
3. The voters/audience will know the credentials and records of all the legally qualified candidates early enough to select the most qualified of those candidates for the final election.
4. The voters/audience will know how, when, and where they can participate in early candidate selection—caucuses, conventions, and primaries.
5. The voters/audience will know the process of campaigning so they can become "media literate" and "politically literate" about the tactics used to win an election.
6. The voters/audience will be allowed to decide for themselves who to elect on election day. No commentator or pollster will preempt this right.
7. The broadcasters will remain independent, not co-opted by candidates, their handlers, or the pollsters.

The method for accomplishing these results is the development of a station election coverage plan. Such a plan will indicate where, when, how, and why the broadcasting techniques discussed in this book can be integrated into existing station programming. Such a plan will establish the tone and the format for coverage, and will build in safeguards against inappropriate judgment calls and biased value judgments.

Reporters will then have a framework within which to do their job. The challenge is to avoid expediency, minimize prejudicial commentary, avoid race and sex bias, and prevent distortion because of inappropriate use of images and symbols. Many opportunities exist for improving coverage by collaborating with colleagues, activating the audience, involving all the candidates, covering the strategies behind each campaign, keeping coverage lively and entertaining as well as substantive, and focusing on the influence money has on politics. For quality work, many professional awards exist. Part of providing quality coverage is to think beyond the quick and dirty sound-bite. For example, at the September 9, 1990 joint, press con-ference of President George Bush and U.S.S.R. President Mikhail Gorbachev, in Helsinki, Gorbachev insisted on answering at length the substance of questions. A number of U.S. reporters were so conditioned to sound-bite replies that they exhibited impatience.

Complete election coverage must address the role of political advertising—the images chosen by a campaign to persuade voters to "buy" their candidate. Ads are more than station revenue. They are costly investments for candidates, carefully and strategically placed. The story behind the ads is one of the most important aspects of campaign coverage.

Not all campaigns involve candidates. Objective coverage of "referenda campaigns" will ensure audiences some interesting, frequently controversial, and exciting coverage of both sides of public policy issues.

A number of tools are available to the broadcaster planning election coverage. Polling is one. Careful use of polling data can enhance one's coverage, but the potential for a station to provide misleading information through polling results is enormous.

Another tool for broadcasters is the technology itself. Much new equipment, such as ENG and SNG, has come onto the market in recent years, making possible forms of election coverage previously not possible. The new equipment provides creative broadcasters with endless opportunities for fitting innovative election coverage into local news programs.

In addition to following the above techniques, if one knows where to get the needed information on government, the offices to which persons will be elected, the laws and regulations affecting elections and election coverage, a station can offer top quality coverage.

Broadcasters, like most professionals, are caught in the web of needing to behave in conventional ways to hold jobs, to get invited to the right cocktail parties, and to advance careers. At the same time prudent innovation is rewarded. The professionals who strive for the six objectives above will be respected innovators who will enhance the bottom line as well as the public service of their station.

Innovation in election coverage can open a world of communication frontiers that redefine both news coverage and the meaning of self-government. It's up to you, the professional at the dawn of the twenty-first century, to learn from the trial and error of recent decades' electronic election coverage, to harness the potential of the new communication technologies and to take as giant a leap forward as our predecessors did when they advanced democratic communication from the town common forum to the first television coverage. You who seize the moment will be the media, political, and government architects of the new century.

Index